The Historical Pirates

Shah Rukh

Published by Shah Rukh, 2024.

While every precaution has been taken in the preparation of this book, the publisher assumes no responsibility for errors or omissions, or for damages resulting from the use of the information contained herein.

THE HISTORICAL PIRATES

First edition. May 30, 2024.

Copyright © 2024 Shah Rukh.

Written by Shah Rukh.

Table of Contents

Prologue

Throughout history, the vast and unpredictable oceans have lured the bold, the desperate, and the adventurous. In their wake, a formidable legacy was forged by those who chose to live by the code of piracy. These men and women, often seen as outlaws, rebels, and villains, were more than mere marauders; they were complex characters driven by ambition, circumstance, and a relentless pursuit of freedom.

From the icy waters of the North Sea to the sun-soaked Caribbean, from the misty Irish coastlines to the bustling ports of the Far East, the stories of pirates have transcended the annals of time, becoming legends that continue to fascinate and intrigue. The Historical Pirates is an exploration into the lives of forty-five such figures, each with a story that contributes to the rich tapestry of maritime history.

Klaus Störtebeker, a notorious German pirate of the late 14th century, opens our journey. Known for his formidable fleet and daring escapades, Störtebeker's tale sets the stage for an era where piracy was as much a statement against oppressive rule as it was a means of survival.

From the rugged coasts of Ireland, Grace O'Malley emerges as a formidable pirate queen, challenging English authority and defying traditional gender roles of the 16th century. Her life, filled with both rebellion and diplomacy, highlights the unique position some pirates held as both outlaws and political figures.

The exploits of Sir Francis Drake, often celebrated as a hero in England but vilified as a pirate by the Spanish, underscore the thin line between piracy and privateering. His story is a testament to the shifting allegiances and moral ambiguities that characterized the Golden Age of Piracy.

Peter Easton, a pirate who once commanded a fleet powerful enough to challenge the navies of Europe, represents the apex of pirate power and influence in the early 17th century. His transition from naval officer to pirate encapsulates the volatile nature of maritime life during this period.

The likes of Roche Braziliano and Henry Morgan bring us to the Caribbean, where piracy flourished in the 17th century. These men, driven by greed, vengeance, and a thirst for adventure, carved out infamous legacies amidst the turquoise waters and treacherous reefs of the New World.

As we move through the chapters, the notorious Blackbeard, the cunning Calico Jack, and the ruthless Bartholomew Roberts emerge as icons of piracy. Their fearsome reputations, bold strategies, and dramatic downfalls paint a vivid picture of a world where life was always on the edge, and death could come with the next wave.

The narratives also include the tales of lesser-known pirates, whose exploits, though not as widely recognized, were equally daring and impactful. From the intrepid Anne Bonny and Mary Read, whose stories challenge the traditional narratives of gender in piracy, to the enigmatic Cheng I Sao, whose command over a vast pirate fleet in the South China Sea remains unparalleled, these figures enrich the complex history of piracy.

The Historical Pirates delves into the lives of these and many more characters, offering a comprehensive look at the diverse and multifaceted world of piracy. Each chapter not only recounts the thrilling adventures and notorious deeds of these pirates but also explores the historical contexts that shaped their lives and legacies.

In this book, you will find tales of treachery and camaraderie, of battles and plunder, of triumph and tragedy. These stories are more than just accounts of crime on the high seas; they are reflections of human nature, driven by the timeless desires for wealth, freedom, and adventure.

Welcome aboard, as we set sail on a journey through the tempestuous seas of history, guided by the daring souls who became legends—the historical pirates.

Chapter 1: Klaus Störtebeker

Klaus Störtebeker, a notorious pirate active during the late 14th century, is a figure shrouded in legend and mystery. His life, although sparsely documented, has been a source of fascination for historians and storytellers alike, weaving a rich tapestry of myth and reality. Born in the 1360s, Störtebeker's exact birthplace remains uncertain, with theories suggesting either Wismar or Hamburg in the Hanseatic League's domain.

Störtebeker, whose real name is believed to be Nikolaus Storzenbecher, earned his moniker from the Low German phrase "Stürz den Becher," meaning "empty the mug in one gulp," a testament to his reputed drinking prowess. As a leader of the Vitalienbrüder, or Victual Brothers, Störtebeker commanded a formidable force of privateers initially commissioned by the Queen of Denmark, Margaret I, to supply provisions to Stockholm during its siege by the forces of Albert of Mecklenburg. However, when the war ended in 1395, the Vitalienbrüder lost their purpose and turned to piracy.

The transition from privateering to outright piracy marked a significant chapter in Störtebeker's life. The Vitalienbrüder, under his leadership, targeted merchant ships of the Hanseatic League, plundering goods and causing substantial disruptions to trade in the Baltic Sea and the North Sea. Störtebeker's fleet was known for its speed and agility, allowing them to elude capture by pursuing naval forces. Their knowledge of the intricate waterways and hidden coves of the North and Baltic Seas provided them with strategic advantages in their piratical endeavors.

Störtebeker's reputation as a pirate was not solely due to his maritime exploits. He was also known for his Robin Hood-like persona, allegedly sharing his plunder with the poor and gaining the support of local populations. This aspect of his legend, while appealing, is difficult to verify historically but has contributed to his enduring legacy as a folk hero.

The Hanseatic League, a powerful commercial and defensive confederation of merchant guilds and market towns in Northwestern and Central Europe, found Störtebeker and his fellow pirates a significant threat to their economic interests. Determined to put an end to the piracy, the League intensified its efforts to capture Störtebeker and dismantle his fleet. Despite several attempts, Störtebeker managed to evade capture for many years, further enhancing his legendary status.

However, his luck eventually ran out. In 1401, a fleet from Hamburg, led by Simon of Utrecht, managed to capture Störtebeker and a significant number of his men near Heligoland. The pirates were taken to Hamburg, where they faced trial and were condemned to death. The method of execution was beheading, a common practice of the time for pirates.

Legend has it that Störtebeker struck a deal with his captors, offering them a gold chain long enough to encircle the city of Hamburg in exchange for his and his men's lives. When this offer was refused, another famous legend emerged from his execution. It is said that Störtebeker requested that all of his men who he could walk past after being beheaded should be spared. According to the tale, after his decapitation, his body allegedly rose and walked past eleven of his men before collapsing. Despite this purported feat, all of his men were executed regardless.

The aftermath of Störtebeker's execution saw his legacy grow rather than diminish. Stories of his exploits and defiance against the Hanseatic League circulated widely, embedding him firmly in maritime lore. His life and death have been romanticized in various forms of literature, theater, and even contemporary media, portraying him as a symbol of resistance against oppressive economic powers.

The historical significance of Klaus Störtebeker extends beyond his piratical activities. His life illustrates the turbulent period of late medieval maritime history, marked by shifting allegiances, economic conflicts, and the thin line between privateering and piracy. The Vitalienbrüder, initially legitimized as privateers, exemplify how quickly such groups could turn to piracy when their official purpose was nullified.

Störtebeker's story also reflects the broader socio-political landscape of the time. The Hanseatic League's dominance in Northern European trade created both wealth and resentment, with pirates like Störtebeker exploiting the discontent among those marginalized by the economic system. His Robin Hood-like image, whether factual or fictional, highlights the social undercurrents and the romanticized notion of the pirate as a champion of the oppressed.

In modern times, Klaus Störtebeker's legacy is commemorated in various ways, particularly in Northern Germany. Festivals, plays, and other cultural events celebrate his life and exploits, keeping the legend alive for new generations. His story continues to captivate the imagination, serving as a reminder of a bygone era of maritime adventure and rebellion.

Chapter 2: Grace O'Malley

Grace O'Malley, known in Irish as Gráinne Mhaol, was born around 1530 into the Gaelic nobility of County Mayo, Ireland. She would grow to become one of the most formidable and legendary figures in Irish history, renowned as a fearless leader, a pirate queen, and a staunch defender of her family's land and autonomy. Her life and legacy straddle the worlds of history and folklore, embodying the fierce independence and resistance of the Irish against English encroachment.

Grace O'Malley was born into the Ó Máille family, one of the dominant seafaring clans in Connacht. Her father, Eoghan Dubhdara Ó Máille, was the chieftain of the clan and controlled significant maritime territory along the western coast of Ireland. From a young age, Grace was exposed to the sea-faring life, developing skills in navigation, sailing, and leadership that would later serve her well. According to legend, when she was young, she begged her father to take her on a trading expedition to Spain. When he refused, citing her gender and the unsuitability of sea life for a girl, she cut off her long hair, earning her the nickname "Gráinne Mhaol" (bald Gráinne) and convincing her father to let her join.

As she grew older, Grace married Dónal an Chogaidh Ó Flaithbheartaigh (Donal of the Battles O'Flaherty), the heir to another powerful seafaring family. Through this marriage, she expanded her influence and command over a substantial fleet of ships and several castles, including Clare Island, a strategically important stronghold. Her husband's frequent absences on raids and battles allowed Grace to assert her authority, commanding her own fleet and conducting her own raids.

Grace's life took a dramatic turn when Dónal was killed in an ambush around 1565. Rather than retreating to a life of widowhood, Grace seized control of the O'Flaherty clan's holdings and continued her maritime activities. She led her fleet in numerous successful raids against rival clans and English ships, earning a fearsome reputation as a pirate queen. Her activities were not solely driven by personal gain but also by a desire to protect her family's territories and maintain Irish sovereignty against increasing English pressure.

By the late 16th century, Grace O'Malley's notoriety had caught the attention of the English authorities in Ireland. Sir Richard Bingham, the English governor of Connacht, viewed her as a significant threat to English rule and sought to curtail her power. Bingham's aggressive policies towards the Irish chieftains included confiscation of lands and suppression of rebellious activities, which naturally put him at odds with Grace. Their conflict reached a peak when Bingham captured and executed her son and heir, Owen, in 1586. This act of cruelty only fueled Grace's determination to resist English encroachment.

One of the most famous episodes in Grace O'Malley's life occurred in 1593, when she decided to seek a direct audience with Queen Elizabeth I to plead for the release of her captured family members and the restoration of her confiscated lands. The meeting between the two formidable women took place at Greenwich Palace. Despite their vastly different backgrounds and the ongoing conflict between their peoples, they reportedly conversed in Latin, finding common ground as women leaders in a male-dominated world. Grace's boldness and eloquence impressed Elizabeth, who agreed to some of her requests, including the release of her son, Tibbot Burke (known as Theobald), and the restoration of some of her lands. However, the concessions were not fully honored by the English officials in Ireland, leading to continued strife.

Throughout her life, Grace O'Malley navigated the complex and often perilous political landscape of 16th-century Ireland. She balanced traditional Gaelic customs and allegiances with the harsh realities of English colonialism. Her ability to lead men in battle, her strategic acumen in maritime warfare, and her diplomatic engagement with the English crown underscore her versatility and resilience. She managed to maintain her clan's independence and protect her interests through a combination of piracy, alliances, and negotiations.

Grace's legacy is a multifaceted one. In the centuries following her death around 1603, she has been remembered as both a ruthless pirate and a valiant patriot. Her story has been romanticized in folklore, songs, and literature, portraying her as a symbol of Irish resistance against foreign domination. Yet, historical records corroborate many of the significant events of her life, painting a picture of a resourceful and determined leader who deftly navigated the turbulent waters of her time.

In Irish cultural memory, Grace O'Malley represents the indomitable spirit of a woman who defied the conventions of her era. Her defiance of gender roles, her leadership in a male-dominated society, and her resistance to English colonization resonate with contemporary audiences. She has been the subject of numerous biographies, academic studies, and creative works, each exploring different facets of her complex persona.

Grace's enduring legacy is also reflected in the places associated with her life. Clare Island, her stronghold, remains a symbol of her power and strategic prowess. The castles she controlled, such as Carrickahowley Castle (now known as Rockfleet Castle), stand as testaments to her influence and the tumultuous times in which she lived.

Chapter 3: Francis Drake

Sir Francis Drake, born around 1540 in Tavistock, Devon, England, is one of the most renowned figures in maritime history. His life was marked by adventure, piracy, exploration, and significant contributions to England's naval dominance. A complex character, Drake's legacy is one of both heroic patriotism and ruthless privateering.

Drake's early life was shaped by the turbulent religious and political climate of 16th-century England. His family, devout Protestants, fled to Kent due to the Catholic persecution under Queen Mary I. This displacement influenced Drake's staunch Protestantism and deep-seated animosity towards Catholic Spain, which would define much of his career. He began his seafaring life as an apprentice on a small coastal vessel owned by his relatives, the Hawkins family, who were prominent in the merchant and privateering businesses.

Drake's first significant voyages were in the service of his cousin, Sir John Hawkins, participating in the highly controversial and lucrative slave trade. These early experiences honed his navigational and combat skills and exposed him to the perils and profits of transatlantic voyages. However, it was an ill-fated expedition to the Caribbean in 1567-1568, where Hawkins and Drake were ambushed by a superior Spanish fleet at San Juan de Ulúa, that cemented Drake's enmity towards Spain. This betrayal by the Spanish, despite a truce agreement, left a lasting impression on Drake and fueled his later exploits against Spanish interests.

Drake's rise to prominence began with his bold raids on Spanish possessions in the Americas. In 1572, he led a successful expedition to capture the Spanish port of Nombre de Dios in present-day Panama. Although the raid did not yield the immense treasure Drake had hoped for, it was notable for his audacious overland march to the Pacific Ocean, where he became the first Englishman to see the Pacific, from a peak in the Isthmus of Panama. This expedition marked the beginning of his reputation as a fearless and cunning privateer.

Drake's most famous voyage was his circumnavigation of the globe from 1577 to 1580. Commissioned by Queen Elizabeth I, Drake set sail with five ships, ostensibly on a trading mission but with secret orders to harass Spanish holdings along the way. After navigating the perilous Strait of Magellan, he ventured up the western coast of South America, capturing Spanish ships and plundering coastal settlements. His most lucrative prize was the Spanish galleon Nuestra Señora de la Concepción, laden with treasure from the Philippines.

Continuing his journey, Drake sailed up the west coast of North America, possibly as far north as present-day Oregon or British Columbia, seeking a navigable route back to the Atlantic. Failing to find the fabled Northwest Passage, he turned south to the coast of California, where he claimed the land for England and named it New Albion. From there, he crossed the Pacific, navigating through the treacherous waters of the Indonesian archipelago, and returned to England via the Cape of Good Hope.

Drake's circumnavigation, completed with only one ship, the Golden Hind, left out of the original five, brought him immense wealth and fame. Queen Elizabeth I knighted him aboard the Golden Hind in 1581, cementing his status as a national hero. His voyage not only demonstrated England's growing naval capabilities but also delivered a severe blow to Spanish prestige and economic power.

In the years following his circumnavigation, Drake continued his privateering activities and played a crucial role in England's naval strategy against Spain. In 1585, tensions between England and Spain escalated, leading to open conflict. Drake was appointed vice admiral of a fleet tasked with preemptive strikes against Spanish ports and shipping. He launched successful raids on Vigo and the Canary Islands before capturing the valuable Spanish port of Santo Domingo in the Caribbean. His most significant achievement during this campaign was the capture of Cartagena de Indias, one of the richest cities in the Spanish New World, although he ultimately failed to capture Havana.

Drake's boldest action came in 1587 when he led a daring raid on the Spanish port of Cadiz, destroying numerous ships and delaying the Spanish Armada's planned invasion of England. This audacious attack, known as the "singeing of the King of Spain's beard," severely hampered Spanish preparations and demonstrated Drake's prowess as a naval commander.

The pinnacle of Drake's naval career came in 1588 with the defeat of the Spanish Armada. As vice admiral under Lord Charles Howard, Drake played a pivotal role in the naval battles that repelled the Spanish fleet. His strategic use of fire ships to scatter the Spanish formation at the Battle of Gravelines was instrumental in securing an English victory. The defeat of the Armada marked a turning point in European history, establishing England as a dominant naval power and heralding the decline of Spanish supremacy.

Despite his successes, Drake's later years were marked by several failures. In 1589, he commanded an expedition to Portugal aimed at capturing Lisbon and fomenting a rebellion against Spanish rule. The expedition was poorly planned and executed, resulting in a humiliating retreat. His final voyage, an ill-fated expedition to the Caribbean in 1595, ended in disaster. Drake's fleet failed to capture San Juan, Puerto Rico, and suffered heavy losses in subsequent encounters with Spanish forces. Weakened by dysentery, Drake died on January 28, 1596, and was buried at sea off the coast of Panama, near the site of his earlier triumphs.

Drake's legacy is a complex one. To the English, he was a national hero, celebrated for his daring exploits and contributions to England's naval supremacy. His circumnavigation of the globe and his role in the defeat of the Spanish Armada earned him a permanent place in the annals of maritime history. However, to the Spanish and many others, he was a ruthless pirate, whose actions caused immense suffering and disruption.

Drake's impact on the course of history extends beyond his immediate achievements. His voyages and raids contributed to the weakening of Spanish control in the Americas and the rise of England as a global maritime power. His exploits inspired future generations of explorers and privateers, laying the groundwork for England's later colonial expansion.

In the broader context of the Age of Exploration, Drake exemplified the era's spirit of adventure, ambition, and ruthless competition. His life story, marked by triumphs and setbacks, embodies the complexities of a period defined by exploration, conquest, and the clash of empires.

Chapter 4: Peter Easton

Peter Easton, born around 1570 in Devon, England, is one of the most successful yet less known pirates in history. His career spanned from being a loyal privateer for the English crown to becoming a notorious pirate who commanded immense power and wealth. Easton's life and legacy illustrate the thin line between state-sanctioned privateering and outright piracy during the volatile maritime conflicts of the late 16th and early 17th centuries.

Easton's early life is shrouded in mystery, with scant records detailing his upbringing. What is known is that he came from a seafaring family in Devon, a region that produced many notable mariners of the era. This background likely provided him with the skills and knowledge necessary for his later exploits on the high seas.

Easton's career began in the service of Queen Elizabeth I of England during the Anglo-Spanish War (1585–1604). As a privateer, Easton was granted a letter of marque, essentially a license to capture enemy ships and goods on behalf of the crown. Privateering was a common practice at the time, allowing nations to augment their naval power with private vessels while disrupting the commerce of their enemies. Easton proved to be an effective and ambitious privateer, quickly gaining a reputation for his prowess and the wealth he accumulated from his captures.

When the Anglo-Spanish War ended with the Treaty of London in 1604, Easton's status as a privateer became precarious. Without the backing of a formal conflict, many privateers found themselves out of work and faced the choice of returning to peaceful pursuits or turning to piracy. Easton chose the latter path, leveraging his experience and resources to build a formidable pirate fleet.

Easton's transition to piracy was seamless, aided by the loyalty of his crew and his existing contacts within the maritime community. He began operating in the waters around Newfoundland, an area rich with

European fishing vessels. The region's remote location and the lack of strong naval presence made it an ideal base for pirate activities. Easton's fleet grew as he captured ships and recruited their crews, amassing a powerful force that dominated the North Atlantic.

One of Easton's most significant achievements was the establishment of a pirate stronghold in Harbour Grace, Newfoundland. Here, he fortified his base, built alliances with local settlers, and created a haven for pirates. Harbour Grace became a thriving hub of pirate activity, where Easton and his men repaired their ships, traded plundered goods, and planned their next raids. The stronghold allowed Easton to exert control over the region, effectively turning it into a pirate enclave.

Easton's operations extended beyond the North Atlantic. He targeted the lucrative shipping lanes of the Caribbean and the eastern coast of North America, capturing merchant vessels and accumulating vast wealth. His success was not merely due to brute force; Easton was a shrewd strategist, often employing tactics of intimidation and negotiation to achieve his aims without unnecessary bloodshed. His reputation grew, and he became one of the most feared and respected pirates of his time.

Despite his success, Easton's career was fraught with challenges. The increasing pressure from European powers to curb piracy led to numerous attempts to capture or eliminate him. However, Easton's naval expertise and the loyalty of his men enabled him to evade capture repeatedly. His ability to navigate the political and military landscape of the time was crucial to his survival.

In 1610, Easton's career took another significant turn. He entered into an alliance with the Barbary corsairs, North African pirates who were a dominant force in the Mediterranean. This alliance expanded Easton's reach and influence, allowing him to operate in new territories and access additional resources. The collaboration with the Barbary corsairs further cemented his status as a major player in the world of piracy.

The turning point in Easton's life came in 1614 when he decided to seek a pardon from the King of France, Louis XIII. Realizing that continued piracy was unsustainable in the face of increasing naval patrols and international pressure, Easton negotiated a deal that would allow him to retire from piracy in exchange for a safe haven and the retention of his wealth. The French king granted him amnesty, and Easton settled in Villefranche-sur-Mer, near Nice, where he lived out his remaining years in comfort and relative obscurity.

Peter Easton's retirement marked the end of a remarkable career that spanned nearly two decades. Unlike many of his contemporaries, who met violent ends, Easton successfully navigated the treacherous waters of piracy and privateering to secure a peaceful retirement. His ability to adapt to changing circumstances, form strategic alliances, and command loyalty set him apart from many other pirates of his era.

Easton's legacy is a testament to the complex and often blurred lines between privateering and piracy. His life story reflects the broader geopolitical and economic forces at play during the late 16th and early 17th centuries, a period marked by intense maritime competition, shifting alliances, and the expansion of European powers into the New World. Easton's success as a pirate can be attributed not only to his naval prowess but also to his keen understanding of these dynamics and his ability to exploit them to his advantage.

Despite his historical significance, Easton remains a relatively obscure figure compared to other famous pirates such as Blackbeard or Henry Morgan. This obscurity may be due in part to the lack of contemporary records and the secretive nature of his operations. Nevertheless, his impact on the maritime history of the North Atlantic and the Caribbean is undeniable, and his story provides valuable insights into the world of piracy during a pivotal era in global history.

In modern times, Peter Easton's legacy has been rediscovered and celebrated in various ways. His exploits have been the subject of historical research, novels, and documentaries, shedding light on his remarkable career and the broader context in which he operated. The town of Harbour Grace, once his pirate stronghold, has embraced its connection to Easton, with local festivals and events commemorating his role in its history.

Peter Easton's life and career epitomize the adventurous and often perilous existence of a pirate. From his beginnings as a loyal privateer to his rise as one of the most powerful pirates in history, Easton's story is one of ambition, adaptability, and resilience. His ability to navigate the shifting tides of fortune and secure a peaceful retirement stands as a unique achievement in the annals of piracy, ensuring that his name endures as a significant, if not widely known, figure in maritime history.

Chapter 5: Roche Braziliano

Roche Braziliano, also known as Rock the Brazilian, was a notorious Dutch pirate who operated in the Caribbean during the mid-17th century. Born around the 1630s in Groningen, Netherlands, he would later become one of the most infamous figures of the buccaneering era. His career is marked by a blend of brutal violence, audacious raids, and significant contributions to the pirate haven of Port Royal, Jamaica.

The early life of Roche Braziliano remains largely obscure, with limited historical records detailing his upbringing. His nickname "Braziliano" suggests that he may have spent considerable time in Brazil, which was a Dutch colony in the early 17th century. This association with Brazil hints at his possible involvement in the lucrative sugar trade or other colonial enterprises before turning to piracy.

Braziliano first emerged in historical records around the 1650s when he joined the ranks of buccaneers in the Caribbean. The buccaneers were a group of privateers and pirates who initially settled on the island of Hispaniola and later expanded their operations throughout the Caribbean. These men were primarily of French, English, and Dutch origin, and they preyed on Spanish shipping and settlements. The constant state of warfare and the lack of strong naval enforcement created a fertile environment for piracy.

Braziliano quickly distinguished himself among the buccaneers for his fearlessness and brutality. One of his earliest recorded exploits was the capture of a Spanish galleon, a feat that not only brought him considerable wealth but also established his reputation as a formidable pirate. Unlike many of his contemporaries who sought to avoid unnecessary bloodshed, Braziliano was known for his ruthlessness. He reportedly tortured and killed prisoners, actions that instilled fear in his enemies and ensured that his name was dreaded along the Spanish Main.

The Spanish Main, the mainland coast of the Spanish Empire in the Americas, was the primary target for Braziliano and his fellow buccaneers. The region was rich with Spanish treasure ships carrying gold, silver, and other valuable commodities back to Europe. These ships, known as flotas, were well-armed and heavily guarded, but the potential rewards were immense. Braziliano's success in attacking these convoys further solidified his status and allowed him to amass significant wealth.

In the mid-1660s, Braziliano made Port Royal, Jamaica, his base of operations. Port Royal was a notorious pirate haven, offering sanctuary and a thriving black market for pirate plunder. The English authorities in Jamaica, seeking to weaken Spanish power in the Caribbean, often turned a blind eye to the pirates' activities. In return, pirates like Braziliano provided valuable intelligence and military support against Spanish incursions.

One of Braziliano's most infamous raids was the attack on the Spanish town of Campeche in 1663. Leading a fleet of buccaneers, he launched a surprise assault on the town, capturing it with relative ease. The raid was marked by extreme violence and looting, with Braziliano and his men plundering the town's wealth and leaving a trail of destruction. This attack exemplified the ferocity and effectiveness of Braziliano's tactics, further enhancing his fearsome reputation.

Despite his successes, Braziliano's brutality and unpredictable nature made him a contentious figure even among his fellow pirates. His willingness to torture and kill prisoners was seen as excessive, and his erratic behavior sometimes endangered his own crew. These traits contributed to his eventual downfall, as his increasingly reckless actions alienated potential allies and made him a target for retaliation.

In 1671, Braziliano's luck ran out. Accounts of his death vary, but it is widely believed that he was captured by Spanish forces and executed. Some stories suggest that he was betrayed by his own men, who had grown weary of his cruelty and instability. Regardless of the exact circumstances, his demise marked the end of a particularly violent chapter in the history of Caribbean piracy.

Roche Braziliano's legacy is a complex one. On one hand, he exemplified the daring and adventurous spirit of the buccaneers, achieving significant successes against Spanish forces and amassing considerable wealth. His raids on Spanish shipping and settlements contributed to the weakening of Spanish control in the Caribbean, a key objective of the buccaneering community.

On the other hand, his extreme violence and cruelty set him apart even among the brutal world of 17th-century piracy. His reputation for torturing and killing prisoners cast a dark shadow over his legacy, and his actions likely fueled the harsh reprisals that pirates often faced from the Spanish authorities. In the broader context of pirate history, Braziliano represents the ruthless edge of buccaneering, where the line between audacious heroism and savage brutality was often blurred.

Braziliano's life and career also highlight the complex relationships between pirates and colonial powers. While pirates were often seen as outlaws and enemies of all nations, they also played a strategic role in the geopolitical conflicts of the era. The English authorities in Jamaica, for instance, tacitly supported Braziliano and other pirates as a means of undermining Spanish dominance in the region. This pragmatic alliance allowed pirates to operate with relative impunity, provided they targeted the common enemy.

The cultural impact of Roche Braziliano extends beyond his lifetime. He has been immortalized in various works of fiction and popular culture, often depicted as the quintessential ruthless pirate. His life story has inspired novels, films, and even video games, contributing to the enduring fascination with the pirate era. These portrayals, while often dramatized, reflect the larger-than-life persona that Braziliano cultivated through his actions and reputation.

In modern scholarship, Braziliano's career offers valuable insights into the social and economic dynamics of piracy in the Caribbean.

His ability to command loyalty and navigate the treacherous waters of pirate politics underscores the complex hierarchies and alliances that characterized pirate communities. Furthermore, his interactions with colonial authorities reveal the shifting power dynamics and the ways in which pirates could exploit geopolitical rivalries to their advantage.

Chapter 6: Henry Morgan

Henry Morgan, born in 1635 in Llanrumney, Monmouthshire, Wales, rose from obscure beginnings to become one of the most renowned privateers and buccaneers of the 17th century. His life, marked by audacious exploits, strategic brilliance, and controversial actions, epitomizes the turbulent world of Caribbean piracy during its golden age. Morgan's career spanned several decades, during which he played a pivotal role in shaping the maritime history of the Caribbean and the power dynamics between European colonial empires.

The early life of Henry Morgan is shrouded in mystery, with conflicting accounts and limited documentation. Some sources suggest that he was the son of a prosperous farmer, while others claim he came from a humbler background. Regardless of his origins, Morgan's path to piracy began in the 1650s when he arrived in the Caribbean. Historical records indicate that he may have initially served as an indentured servant in Barbados, a common fate for many young men seeking fortunes in the New World. However, Morgan soon gravitated towards the life of a privateer, driven by the promise of wealth and adventure.

Morgan's early career was closely tied to the buccaneering community of Port Royal, Jamaica. Established by the English as a base for privateering, Port Royal quickly became a notorious haven for pirates, offering sanctuary and a thriving black market for plundered goods. The English crown tacitly supported privateers like Morgan, who targeted Spanish shipping and settlements, thereby weakening Spain's dominance in the region. This pragmatic alliance between privateers and colonial authorities provided the backdrop for Morgan's rise to prominence.

Morgan's first significant venture was his participation in the capture of Santiago de Cuba in 1662. This raid, led by Christopher Myngs, was a precursor to the large-scale operations that would define

Morgan's career. His courage and leadership during the assault earned him recognition and the command of his own vessel. Morgan's tactical acumen and ability to inspire loyalty among his men quickly set him apart from other privateers.

By the mid-1660s, Morgan had emerged as a leading figure among the buccaneers. His most famous exploits during this period involved a series of daring raids on Spanish strongholds. In 1668, he led a successful assault on Puerto Príncipe (modern-day Camagüey, Cuba), a raid characterized by its boldness and meticulous planning. Morgan and his men infiltrated the town under cover of darkness, overwhelming the defenders and seizing a substantial amount of treasure. This victory bolstered Morgan's reputation and solidified his position as one of the most formidable privateers in the Caribbean.

Morgan's audacity reached new heights with his subsequent raid on Portobelo, Panama, in 1668. This operation demonstrated his strategic brilliance and ruthlessness. Morgan's fleet approached the heavily fortified town at night, and his men launched a surprise attack at dawn. Despite facing fierce resistance, Morgan's forces overcame the defenders, capturing the town and its wealth. The fall of Portobelo sent shockwaves throughout the Spanish Empire, showcasing Morgan's ability to strike at the heart of Spanish power in the Americas.

Morgan's exploits earned him both admiration and notoriety. While the English authorities in Jamaica celebrated his successes, the Spanish viewed him as a ruthless pirate and a significant threat. The capture of Portobelo prompted the Spanish to intensify their efforts to defend their territories and retaliate against the buccaneers. However, Morgan's strategic acumen and the support he received from Port Royal allowed him to continue his operations with relative impunity.

In 1670, Morgan embarked on what would become his most famous and controversial expedition: the attack on Panama City. This campaign, meticulously planned and executed, remains one of the most audacious feats in the history of piracy. Morgan assembled a fleet of over thirty ships and a force of nearly two thousand men, including English, French, and Dutch buccaneers. Setting sail from Jamaica, they first captured the island of Santa Catalina, securing a base of operations. From there, they moved to the mainland, capturing the fortress of San Lorenzo at the mouth of the Chagres River.

The march to Panama City was grueling, as Morgan's men traversed dense jungles and faced fierce resistance from Spanish forces. Despite these challenges, Morgan's leadership and determination prevailed. On January 28, 1671, his forces launched a surprise attack on Panama City, overwhelming the defenders and capturing the city. The ensuing sacking of Panama City was brutal, with widespread looting and destruction. The city was set ablaze, and much of its wealth was seized by Morgan and his men.

The attack on Panama City was a significant blow to Spanish prestige and power in the Americas. However, it also brought Morgan into conflict with the English crown. The attack occurred during a period of tentative peace between England and Spain, and Morgan's actions threatened to disrupt diplomatic relations. In response, the English authorities in Jamaica arrested Morgan and sent him to England to face charges of piracy.

Despite these charges, Morgan's fortunes took a dramatic turn upon his arrival in England. King Charles II, recognizing Morgan's achievements and the strategic importance of his actions, pardoned him and knighted him in 1674. Morgan's knighthood marked a remarkable transformation from a feared pirate to a respected gentleman. He returned to Jamaica as Lieutenant Governor, tasked with maintaining order and defending the colony against external threats.

As Lieutenant Governor, Morgan faced the complex challenge of balancing his duties with his past as a buccaneer. His tenure was marked by efforts to suppress piracy, reflecting the shifting priorities of the English crown. However, Morgan's efforts were complicated by his own connections to the pirate community and the enduring influence of buccaneers in Port Royal. Despite these challenges, he managed to maintain a degree of stability and order in the colony.

In his later years, Morgan's health declined, exacerbated by his hard-living lifestyle and the tropical climate of Jamaica. He continued to play a role in colonial administration until his death in 1688. Morgan was buried with full honors in Port Royal, a testament to his lasting impact on the colony and his complex legacy.

Henry Morgan's life and career offer a fascinating glimpse into the world of 17th-century piracy and the geopolitical dynamics of the Caribbean. His ability to navigate the shifting tides of fortune, from privateer to pirate to colonial administrator, underscores the fluid boundaries between legality and illegality during this era. Morgan's strategic brilliance, audacity, and adaptability enabled him to achieve remarkable successes and secure a place in history as one of the most iconic figures of the golden age of piracy.

Morgan's legacy is multifaceted, encompassing both his contributions to English colonial expansion and his reputation as a ruthless pirate. To the English, he was a hero who dealt significant blows to Spanish power and enriched the coffers of the empire. To the Spanish, he was a scourge, a symbol of the lawlessness and brutality that plagued their colonies. This duality is reflected in the way Morgan is remembered in history and popular culture.

In the centuries following his death, Morgan's exploits have been romanticized and mythologized, contributing to the enduring fascination with pirate lore. His life has inspired numerous books, films, and television series, cementing his status as a larger-than-life figure. Despite the embellishments and fictionalizations, the core of Morgan's story remains a testament to the extraordinary impact one individual can have on the course of history.

In modern scholarship, Morgan's career is studied as part of the broader context of European colonialism and the economic and political forces that shaped the Caribbean. His actions are seen as both a reflection of and a response to the intense competition for resources and territory among European powers. Morgan's ability to exploit these dynamics to his advantage highlights the complex interplay between piracy, privateering, and state power during this period.

Henry Morgan's life and legacy continue to captivate and intrigue, providing valuable insights into the tumultuous world of 17th-century piracy. His story, marked by adventure, conflict, and transformation, remains a compelling chapter in the history of the Caribbean and the broader narrative of the age of exploration and empire.

Chapter 7: François l'Olonnais

François l'Olonnais, born Jean-David Nau around 1635 in Les Sables-d'Olonne, France, was one of the most notorious and brutal pirates of the 17th century. His life was marked by extreme violence, audacious raids, and a relentless pursuit of wealth, all of which earned him a fearsome reputation among both his contemporaries and posterity. His career exemplifies the brutal and chaotic world of Caribbean piracy during the golden age of buccaneering.

Little is known about Nau's early life in France, but like many young men of his time, he was likely drawn to the Caribbean by the promise of adventure and fortune. He arrived in the West Indies as an indentured servant, a common practice that allowed impoverished Europeans to pay for their passage to the New World in exchange for several years of labor. By the time his servitude ended, Nau had adopted the moniker l'Olonnais, a nod to his place of origin, and he soon turned to piracy, joining the ranks of the buccaneers based in Tortuga and Hispaniola.

The buccaneers were a motley crew of adventurers, escaped slaves, and former soldiers who initially hunted wild cattle and hogs on Hispaniola before turning to piracy. Their early targets were primarily Spanish ships and settlements, as Spain was the dominant colonial power in the Caribbean. The buccaneers operated under the tacit approval of other European powers, such as France and England, who were eager to weaken Spanish influence in the region.

L'Olonnais quickly distinguished himself among the buccaneers for his exceptional cruelty and daring. His first major raid was in 1660 when he and his crew captured a Spanish ship off the coast of Cuba. After slaughtering the entire crew, l'Olonnais used the ship to launch a series of attacks along the coast, targeting Spanish towns and vessels. His ruthlessness became legendary; he was known to torture captives for information and then kill them in gruesome ways, earning him a reputation as one of the most feared pirates in the Caribbean.

In 1663, l'Olonnais led a raid on the town of Campeche on the Yucatán Peninsula. This assault demonstrated his strategic acumen and his willingness to employ extreme measures to achieve his goals. Despite facing stiff resistance, l'Olonnais and his men captured the town, looting its wealth and taking many prisoners. The raid on Campeche further cemented his fearsome reputation and marked the beginning of his most infamous period of activity.

L'Olonnais' next major exploit was the capture of Maracaibo and Gibraltar in Venezuela in 1666. He led a fleet of eight ships and a crew of 650 buccaneers, attacking and sacking both towns with unparalleled brutality. The raid on Maracaibo was particularly savage; l'Olonnais' men tortured and killed hundreds of residents in their search for hidden treasure. The town of Gibraltar met a similar fate, with its inhabitants subjected to horrific violence.

These raids were not only lucrative but also served as a stark warning to other Spanish settlements in the region. L'Olonnais' reputation for cruelty ensured that many towns surrendered without a fight, preferring to negotiate terms rather than face his wrath. His ability to instill fear in his enemies was one of his greatest assets, allowing him to achieve significant successes with relatively small forces.

However, l'Olonnais' reign of terror was not without setbacks. His fleet often faced challenges such as storms, diseases, and shortages of supplies. In one instance, his ship was wrecked off the coast of Campeche, and he and his surviving crew were forced to make their way through hostile Spanish territory. Despite being pursued by Spanish soldiers, l'Olonnais managed to evade capture, displaying his resourcefulness and tenacity.

The turning point in l'Olonnais' career came in 1667 when he planned an ambitious raid on the rich Spanish province of Nicaragua.

He assembled a fleet of ten ships and a crew of over 700 men, aiming to capture the city of San Pedro. However, the expedition faced numerous difficulties from the outset. The fleet encountered severe storms, and several ships were lost. Those that survived were scattered, and the remaining crew members were plagued by illness and shortages of food and water.

Undeterred, l'Olonnais pressed on with his diminished forces, capturing the town of San Pedro and torturing its inhabitants to extract information about hidden treasures. The brutality of the raid shocked even his fellow buccaneers, who were accustomed to violence. However, the treasure l'Olonnais sought eluded him, as the residents had hidden much of their wealth or fled before his arrival.

Following the raid on San Pedro, l'Olonnais' fortunes began to decline. His fleet, weakened by losses and the rigors of the expedition, was less effective in subsequent raids. In 1668, l'Olonnais led a raid on the Gulf of Honduras, targeting the town of Puerto Caballos. The raid was a disaster; l'Olonnais and his men were ambushed by Spanish forces and suffered heavy casualties. The few survivors, including l'Olonnais, retreated into the jungle.

L'Olonnais' fate was sealed when he and his remaining crew encountered a band of hostile indigenous people, the Kuna, in the Darién region of Panama. According to legend, the Kuna captured l'Olonnais and his men, killed them, and dismembered their bodies. The grisly details of his death are uncertain, but it is widely accepted that he met a violent end, fitting for a pirate whose life was marked by extreme brutality.

François l'Olonnais' legacy is one of terror and infamy. His willingness to employ torture and violence set him apart from other pirates of his time, and his name became synonymous with cruelty. While his actions earned him a considerable fortune and a fearsome reputation, they also ensured that he was one of the most hated and hunted men in the Caribbean.

L'Olonnais' career reflects the chaotic and brutal nature of Caribbean piracy in the 17th century. The buccaneers operated in a world where loyalty was fleeting, and survival often depended on one's ability to instill fear and ruthlessly eliminate rivals. L'Olonnais' success as a pirate can be attributed to his tactical brilliance, his ability to inspire fear, and his relentless pursuit of wealth. However, his extreme cruelty ultimately isolated him from potential allies and made him a target for retribution.

In historical memory, l'Olonnais stands out as one of the most violent figures of the golden age of piracy. His raids on Spanish towns and ships contributed to the weakening of Spanish control in the Caribbean, a key objective of the buccaneers. However, his legacy is also a reminder of the darker aspects of piracy, where the pursuit of treasure often came at the cost of human suffering and destruction.

L'Olonnais' life has been romanticized and mythologized in various works of fiction, contributing to the enduring fascination with pirate lore. His story, marked by adventure, brutality, and eventual downfall, continues to captivate and intrigue, providing a stark contrast to the more romanticized portrayals of pirates in popular culture. In the broader context of maritime history, François l'Olonnais remains a symbol of the extreme violence and lawlessness that characterized the era of Caribbean buccaneering.

Chapter 8: Thomas Tew

Thomas Tew, often referred to as the "Rhode Island Pirate," was a notorious pirate and privateer who operated in the late 17th century. His life and career are emblematic of the golden age of piracy, a time when pirates roamed the seas with impunity, plundering ships and settlements and often blurring the lines between legitimate privateering and outright piracy. Born around 1649, likely in Newport, Rhode Island, Tew's exploits and adventures made him one of the most famous pirates of his era, and his legacy has endured in both historical accounts and popular culture.

The early life of Thomas Tew is not well-documented, but it is generally believed that he was born into a respectable family in Newport, Rhode Island. Newport was a bustling colonial port, and it is likely that Tew was exposed to maritime life from a young age. By the 1690s, Tew had established himself as a privateer, a profession that involved attacking and capturing enemy ships under the authorization of a government-issued letter of marque. Privateering was a legal form of piracy, sanctioned by governments during times of war to weaken their enemies' shipping and commerce.

In 1692, Tew embarked on a privateering venture that would set the course for his notorious career. He obtained a letter of marque from the governor of Bermuda, ostensibly to attack French ships and settlements along the West African coast. However, Tew had other plans. Along with a small but determined crew, he set sail aboard his ship, the Amity, not towards the designated targets but instead towards the rich and relatively undefended shipping lanes of the Indian Ocean. This decision marked Tew's transition from privateer to pirate.

Tew's voyage to the Indian Ocean was fraught with peril, but his gamble paid off spectacularly. In 1693, he encountered an Indian ship, the Fateh Muhammed, laden with treasure. Tew and his crew attacked the vessel, and after a fierce battle, they overpowered its defenders and captured the ship. The haul was enormous, with reports suggesting that Tew's share alone amounted to over £100,000, a fortune at the time. This successful raid made Tew and his crew incredibly wealthy and cemented his reputation as a daring and successful pirate.

Flush with success, Tew returned to Newport, where he was greeted as a hero. The colonial authorities, who were often ambivalent about piracy, turned a blind eye to Tew's activities, likely due to the wealth he brought back to the colony. Encouraged by his success and the lack of repercussions, Tew decided to embark on another voyage to the Indian Ocean. This second expedition, however, would prove to be his last.

In 1694, Tew set sail again on the Amity, this time with a larger crew and even grander ambitions. He aimed to replicate the success of his previous raid by targeting the lucrative shipping routes of the Indian Ocean once more. This time, he was joined by other notorious pirates, including Henry Every, forming what became known as the "Pirate Round." The Pirate Round was a route taken by pirates from the Americas to the Indian Ocean, where they preyed on the rich merchant ships of the Mughal Empire and other trading nations.

Tew's second voyage initially mirrored the success of his first. He continued to capture valuable prizes, enriching himself and his crew. However, in 1695, his luck ran out. While attacking a Mughal convoy near the Arabian Peninsula, Tew engaged in a fierce battle with one of the convoy's escort ships. During the skirmish, Tew was mortally wounded, reportedly by a cannonball that tore through his abdomen. He died shortly thereafter, and with his death, his crew disbanded, and the Amity was abandoned.

The death of Thomas Tew marked the end of one of the most colorful and influential pirate careers of the late 17th century. Tew's legacy, however, continued to influence the world of piracy. His daring raids and the immense wealth he accumulated inspired countless other pirates to follow in his footsteps. The success of Tew and his contemporaries in the Indian Ocean highlighted the vulnerability of the rich trade routes and the potential rewards for those bold enough to seize them.

Tew's career also had significant implications for the colonial powers of the time. His activities, along with those of other pirates operating in the Indian Ocean, disrupted the lucrative trade between Europe and Asia, leading to increased efforts by the British, French, and Dutch to suppress piracy. The actions of Tew and his fellow pirates prompted the British East India Company and other trading companies to fortify their ships and improve their naval defenses, leading to a protracted struggle between pirates and the navies of the colonial powers.

Despite his relatively short career, Thomas Tew left an indelible mark on the history of piracy. His exploits were widely reported and became part of pirate lore, contributing to the romanticized image of the swashbuckling pirate in popular culture. Tew's life has been the subject of numerous books, articles, and even films, cementing his place in the pantheon of legendary pirates.

In addition to his direct impact on piracy and trade, Tew's life offers valuable insights into the broader social and economic context of the late 17th century. His ability to move between the worlds of legitimate privateering and outright piracy reflects the fluid and often ambiguous nature of maritime law and order during this period. The willingness of colonial authorities to tolerate or even tacitly support pirate activities when it suited their interests underscores the complex relationships between pirates, privateers, and the colonial governments.

Tew's career also highlights the interconnected nature of the global economy in the 17th century. His raids on Indian and Mughal ships illustrate the far-reaching impact of European colonial expansion and the extent to which global trade networks had developed by this time. The wealth Tew plundered from these ships was part of a vast web of commerce that linked Asia, Africa, Europe, and the Americas, and his actions had ripple effects throughout this global system.

In examining Tew's legacy, it is important to consider both the myth and the reality of his life. While the romantic image of the daring pirate adventurer has enduring appeal, the reality of Tew's career was marked by violence, danger, and the ruthless pursuit of wealth. His willingness to abandon the constraints of privateering for the greater rewards of piracy underscores the precarious and often brutal nature of life on the high seas during this era.

Ultimately, Thomas Tew's story is a testament to the allure and peril of piracy in the golden age of piracy. His bold exploits, dramatic rise to wealth, and untimely death encapsulate the volatile and dangerous world of the 17th-century pirate. As a historical figure, Tew continues to captivate and intrigue, offering a window into a turbulent and transformative period in maritime history. His life and legacy, marked by adventure, violence, and the relentless pursuit of fortune, remain a fascinating chapter in the annals of piracy.

Chapter 9: William Kidd

Captain William Kidd, born in Dundee, Scotland, around 1645, is one of the most infamous figures of the golden age of piracy. His story is a complex tale of ambition, betrayal, and a dramatic fall from grace, intertwining piracy with privateering and political intrigue. Kidd's life and career have been the subject of extensive historical scrutiny, mythologizing, and debate, making him a pivotal character in maritime history.

Kidd's early life remains somewhat obscure, but it is believed he came from a modest background. His father, a seafarer, died at sea when Kidd was young, which likely influenced his future career on the ocean. By the 1680s, Kidd had established himself as a successful privateer, operating out of the Caribbean. Privateers were licensed by governments to attack enemy ships during wartime, blurring the line between legitimate naval warfare and piracy.

In 1689, Kidd's privateering efforts garnered him significant acclaim. He commanded a privateer ship commissioned by the English government during the Nine Years' War against France. His success in capturing French vessels earned him a reputation as a skilled and reliable seaman. During this period, Kidd married Sarah Bradley Cox Oort, a wealthy widow, which further elevated his social standing and provided him with valuable connections.

Kidd's most famous voyage began in 1696, when he received a commission from the Earl of Bellomont, who was then the Governor of New York and Massachusetts Bay. The commission was intended to authorize Kidd to hunt down and capture pirates preying on English shipping in the Indian Ocean. This venture was backed by prominent investors, including several influential members of the English government. Kidd's mission was not only to eliminate piracy but also to seize any valuable goods from captured pirate ships, which would be shared among the investors.

Kidd's ship, the Adventure Galley, was a state-of-the-art vessel equipped with 34 cannons and a crew of around 150 men. Setting sail from London in 1696, Kidd's journey to the Indian Ocean was fraught with challenges. His crew became increasingly unruly, and tensions ran high as the voyage dragged on without significant success. The lack of pirate targets and mounting frustration led to several mutinous incidents among his men.

The turning point in Kidd's career came with the capture of the Quedagh Merchant, an Armenian ship sailing under a French pass. This vessel, laden with valuable cargo, was a lucrative prize, but its seizure marked the beginning of Kidd's downfall. The ambiguous legality of the capture – as the ship was owned by Indian merchants but sailed under a French flag – left Kidd vulnerable to accusations of piracy. Despite his protestations that he was operating under his commission, the capture of the Quedagh Merchant was seen as an act of piracy by both his crew and his investors back in England.

Kidd's troubles escalated when he made port at the island of Saint Marie off Madagascar. Here, he encountered the notorious pirate Robert Culliford, whose crew defected to Culliford, leaving Kidd with a skeleton crew. Desperate and isolated, Kidd abandoned the Adventure Galley, which had become unseaworthy, and sailed back to the Caribbean on the Quedagh Merchant, now renamed the Adventure Prize.

By the time Kidd returned to the Americas in 1699, the political landscape had changed dramatically. The anti-pirate sentiment had intensified, and news of his exploits – particularly the capture of the Quedagh Merchant – had reached the authorities. Kidd sailed to New York, hoping to clear his name with the help of his influential backers, including the Earl of Bellomont. However, he was arrested and sent to England to stand trial.

Kidd's trial in 1701 was a sensational affair, capturing public attention and drawing significant media coverage. He faced multiple charges of piracy and murder, including the killing of his gunner, William Moore, during a mutiny. Kidd's defense hinged on the legitimacy of his privateering commission and the claim that he had only attacked ships that were lawful targets. However, the political climate and the interests of his powerful backers worked against him. The evidence against Kidd was compelling, and he was ultimately found guilty of piracy and murder.

On May 23, 1701, William Kidd was executed by hanging at Execution Dock in Wapping, London. His body was gibbeted – displayed in an iron cage – on the River Thames as a grim warning to other would-be pirates. The gruesome display underscored the seriousness with which the British authorities sought to stamp out piracy and reassert control over their maritime interests.

Despite his ignominious end, Kidd's legacy has endured in both historical and popular narratives. The ambiguity surrounding his actions, the political machinations that contributed to his downfall, and the vast treasure he was rumored to have buried have all contributed to his lasting infamy. The legend of Captain Kidd's buried treasure has inspired countless treasure hunts and literary works, cementing his place in the pantheon of pirate lore.

Historians continue to debate the extent to which Kidd was a pirate versus a privateer caught in a web of political intrigue. His case highlights the thin line between lawful privateering and piracy, particularly in an era when the rules of engagement on the high seas were often murky and subject to change based on political expediency. Kidd's downfall can be seen as a cautionary tale about the risks and complexities of privateering, where the fortunes of a sea captain could turn on a dime based on shifting political winds and the interpretations of distant authorities.

The narrative of Captain Kidd also provides insight into the broader context of piracy and privateering in the late 17th and early 18th centuries. The era was marked by intense maritime competition among European powers, and the use of privateers was a common strategy to disrupt enemy shipping and commerce. Privateering was a double-edged sword, offering the promise of great rewards but also the risk of crossing into piracy, with severe consequences for those who fell afoul of the law.

Kidd's life and career reflect the volatile nature of this period, where fortunes were made and lost on the high seas, and where the boundaries between hero and villain were often blurred. His story is a testament to the daring and ambition of those who sought their fortunes through privateering, as well as the harsh realities faced by those who navigated the treacherous waters of political and legal uncertainty.

In addition to his place in history as a pirate, Kidd's legacy has influenced popular culture in significant ways. He has been the subject of numerous books, films, and other media, often portrayed as the quintessential swashbuckling pirate. The allure of his rumored buried treasure has inspired countless treasure hunts and continues to capture the imagination of adventurers and storytellers alike. The enduring fascination with Captain Kidd speaks to the timeless appeal of pirate legends and the complex interplay between history and myth.

Chapter 10: Nicholas Van Hoorn

Nicholas Van Hoorn was a notorious pirate during the Golden Age of Piracy, whose exploits and adventures have left a lasting mark on the annals of maritime history. Born around 1635 in the Spanish Netherlands, which is present-day Belgium, Van Hoorn's early life remains somewhat obscure, with few records detailing his formative years. However, his subsequent career as a pirate would become well-documented through various accounts and chronicles of the time.

Van Hoorn first emerged in historical records in the mid-17th century, a period characterized by intense colonial rivalry and frequent naval warfare among European powers. This environment provided fertile ground for privateers and pirates to thrive, and Van Hoorn quickly capitalized on the opportunities it presented. Initially, he operated as a privateer, a legal pirate sanctioned by a government to attack enemy ships during wartime. His early endeavors were likely under the employ of the Dutch Republic, a maritime power frequently at odds with Spain, England, and France.

Transitioning from privateer to outright pirate, Van Hoorn began targeting vessels indiscriminately, driven by the lure of greater profits and freedom from government oversight. By the early 1680s, he had established himself as a formidable pirate commander, known for his ruthlessness and strategic acumen. His operations extended across the Caribbean Sea, a hotspot for piracy due to its rich trade routes and relatively weak colonial defenses.

One of Van Hoorn's most notable ventures occurred in 1682 when he and fellow pirate Michel de Grammont launched a daring raid on the Spanish city of Veracruz in present-day Mexico. The attack was meticulously planned and executed with brutal efficiency. Van Hoorn and his men infiltrated the city under the cover of darkness, overwhelming the Spanish defenders and looting the city's wealth. The raid on Veracruz not only enriched Van Hoorn and his crew but also cemented his reputation as a masterful and daring pirate leader.

Despite his success, Van Hoorn's piratical career was marked by a volatile temperament and a penchant for violence that often strained his relationships with other pirates. This volatility came to a head in 1683, during an expedition against the Spanish stronghold of Campeche. Van Hoorn had joined forces with the infamous pirate Laurens de Graaf for the assault. The partnership between Van Hoorn and de Graaf was uneasy, plagued by mutual distrust and conflicting egos.

The tension between the two came to a tragic conclusion when Van Hoorn, in a fit of rage, killed several Spanish prisoners who had surrendered under the promise of quarter. This act of brutality horrified de Graaf and the other pirates, who valued their reputation and the potential for future surrenders based on their perceived honor. In retaliation for this breach of conduct, de Graaf and the crew turned on Van Hoorn, severely wounding him in a skirmish that erupted on the decks of their ships.

Van Hoorn's injuries proved fatal, and he died shortly after the confrontation in 1683. His death marked the end of a turbulent and violent career that had spanned several decades and left a lasting impact on the history of piracy. Despite his relatively short life, Nicholas Van Hoorn's exploits epitomized the chaotic and brutal nature of piracy during the Golden Age. His story reflects the complexities of pirate society, where alliances were fragile, and the line between lawful privateering and outright piracy was often blurred.

Van Hoorn's legacy lives on in the numerous accounts and legends that have immortalized his name. His life serves as a testament to the daring and often destructive spirit of the pirates who roamed the Caribbean and beyond, challenging the naval powers of their time and carving out a violent and tumultuous existence on the high seas. Today, he is remembered not just for his daring raids and fierce battles but also for the volatile and uncompromising nature that ultimately led to his demise.

Chapter 11: Edward Teach

Edward Teach, more commonly known as Blackbeard, is one of the most infamous pirates in history. His name has become synonymous with the Golden Age of Piracy, a period from the late 17th to early 18th centuries when piracy was rampant in the Caribbean and along the eastern seaboard of North America. Teach's fearsome reputation, dramatic appearance, and daring exploits have made him a legendary figure whose story has captivated imaginations for centuries.

Edward Teach was likely born around 1680 in Bristol, England, though details of his early life remain sparse and speculative. Some historical records suggest that he may have come from a relatively respectable family and that he possibly served as a sailor or privateer during Queen Anne's War (1702-1713). Privateering, which involved attacking enemy ships with the government's blessing, provided many future pirates with the skills and experience they later used in their piratical careers.

By the early 1710s, Teach had abandoned any semblance of lawful privateering and had turned to outright piracy. His rise to prominence began under the mentorship of Benjamin Hornigold, a well-known pirate captain operating out of the Caribbean. Teach served as Hornigold's subordinate and quickly proved his prowess and leadership abilities. When Hornigold retired from piracy around 1717, Teach took command of his own vessel, marking the beginning of his legendary career.

Teach's most famous ship was the Queen Anne's Revenge, a former French slave ship he captured and heavily armed with up to 40 guns. The sight of this formidable vessel, combined with Teach's terrifying persona, struck fear into the hearts of sailors and merchants across the region. Teach's appearance was carefully cultivated to enhance his fearsome reputation. He was known for his tall stature, dark, thick beard, and menacing eyes. During battles, he would tie slow-burning fuses into his beard and light them, creating a hellish image with smoke and flames surrounding his face. This dramatic and intimidating image, coupled with his ruthless tactics, ensured that many ships surrendered without a fight when confronted by Blackbeard.

One of Blackbeard's most notable exploits was the blockade of Charleston, South Carolina, in May 1718. Teach and his fleet captured several ships attempting to enter or leave the harbor, effectively sealing off the city. He then sent an emissary to demand a chest of medicine from the local government, threatening to kill the captured prisoners and burn the ships if his demands were not met. After several days of tense negotiations, the city complied, and Blackbeard released his captives and sailed away with the medicine.

Following the Charleston blockade, Blackbeard sailed north to the coast of North Carolina, where he ran the Queen Anne's Revenge aground near Beaufort Inlet. Whether this was an accident or a deliberate act to downsize his crew and share less of his plunder remains a matter of speculation. Blackbeard and his most loyal men escaped with the valuables, leaving the stranded crew to fend for themselves.

In the summer of 1718, Blackbeard accepted a royal pardon from Governor Charles Eden of North Carolina, who was known to be sympathetic to pirates. For a short time, Teach settled down in Bath, North Carolina, seemingly enjoying a peaceful life. However, it was not long before he returned to piracy, unable or unwilling to abandon the life of plunder and adventure. He resumed his activities, attacking ships along the American coast and in the Caribbean.

Blackbeard's renewed piracy caught the attention of Alexander Spotswood, the Governor of Virginia. Spotswood, determined to put an end to Blackbeard's reign of terror, dispatched Lieutenant Robert Maynard of the Royal Navy to hunt him down. On November 22, 1718, Maynard and his men caught up with Blackbeard near Ocracoke Island, North Carolina. In a fierce and bloody battle, Maynard's forces boarded Blackbeard's ship. Teach fought valiantly but was ultimately overpowered and killed. His body was reportedly struck with at least five gunshots and twenty sword wounds before he fell. As a grim warning to other pirates, Maynard had Blackbeard's head cut off and displayed on the bowsprit of his ship.

Blackbeard's death marked the end of one of the most dramatic and colorful careers in the annals of piracy. His exploits had become the stuff of legend even before his demise, and his fearsome reputation ensured his place in history. Over the years, Blackbeard has been romanticized in books, movies, and folklore, often depicted as the quintessential pirate with a heart of gold beneath his ruthless exterior.

The mythos surrounding Blackbeard often overshadows the reality of his life. While he was undoubtedly a ruthless and cunning pirate, many of the more sensational stories about him are likely exaggerations or fabrications. Nonetheless, Blackbeard's impact on the history of piracy is undeniable. He represents the height of the pirate threat during the early 18th century and the complex interplay between piracy, colonial politics, and commerce.

Historians continue to study Blackbeard's life and the broader context of the Golden Age of Piracy to better understand the economic, social, and political factors that allowed piracy to flourish during this period. Blackbeard's ability to navigate the treacherous waters of piracy and evade capture for so long speaks to his skill as a seafarer and his understanding of the political landscape of the time.

Edward Teach, or Blackbeard, remains a symbol of the pirate era—a larger-than-life figure whose name still evokes images of adventure, danger, and the relentless quest for freedom on the high seas. His life and legacy continue to be a source of fascination and intrigue, embodying the enduring allure of the pirate's life.

Chapter 12: John Rackham

John Rackham, better known as Calico Jack, is a prominent figure in the annals of piracy, his legacy defined by his flamboyant personality, distinctive fashion sense, and association with two of the most famous female pirates, Anne Bonny and Mary Read. Born around 1682, likely in England, Rackham's early life remains largely undocumented, leaving much of his formative years to speculation. His epithet "Calico Jack" derives from his preference for colorful calico clothing, which set him apart from his peers and contributed to his enduring image in popular culture.

Rackham first emerges in historical records as a quartermaster under the infamous pirate captain Charles Vane. The early 18th century, a period known as the Golden Age of Piracy, saw the Caribbean and the eastern coast of North America teeming with pirate activity. Vane and his crew, including Rackham, operated primarily in this region, attacking and plundering merchant vessels. As quartermaster, Rackham was responsible for maintaining order on the ship, distributing provisions, and overseeing the division of loot—a role that underscored his leadership qualities and earned him respect among the crew.

Calico Jack's career as a pirate captain began in November 1718 following a dramatic mutiny against Charles Vane. Vane's refusal to engage a French warship—a decision motivated by the ship's superior firepower—led to discontent among the crew. Seizing the moment, Rackham rallied the dissatisfied pirates and successfully ousted Vane, who was left on a small sloop with a handful of loyal followers. Rackham was subsequently elected captain, marking the beginning of his independent command.

As captain, Rackham's tenure was marked by a combination of audacity and opportunism. He preferred smaller, faster ships, which allowed him to execute quick, surprise attacks on merchant vessels.

His primary hunting grounds included the waters of the Bahamas and Cuba, areas with bustling trade routes that provided ample targets for plunder. Rackham's strategic acumen and charismatic leadership earned him a reputation among his peers, although his exploits were often overshadowed by those of more notorious contemporaries like Blackbeard and Bartholomew Roberts.

One of the most significant aspects of Rackham's pirate career was his partnership with Anne Bonny, a fierce and independent woman who defied the gender norms of the time. Bonny, originally from Ireland, had eloped to the Bahamas with her husband but soon became enamored with the pirate lifestyle and, specifically, with Rackham. She left her husband to join Rackham at sea, disguising herself as a man to gain acceptance among the crew. Anne Bonny's presence on Rackham's ship was unconventional and scandalous, reflecting the rebellious spirit of the pirate world.

In 1720, another remarkable pirate joined Rackham's crew: Mary Read. Like Bonny, Read had also disguised herself as a man to navigate the male-dominated world of piracy. Her path to piracy began with a life of disguise; she had spent much of her early life posing as a boy to gain access to opportunities otherwise denied to women. Her seafaring skills and bravery soon became apparent, and she quickly became an integral part of Rackham's crew. The presence of two female pirates on Rackham's ship was unprecedented and became a defining feature of his legacy.

Rackham, Bonny, and Read formed a formidable trio, and their exploits became legendary. They engaged in numerous acts of piracy, capturing several vessels and accumulating considerable loot. The dynamic between the three, particularly the fierce loyalty and camaraderie shared by Bonny and Read, added a unique dimension to Rackham's pirate endeavors. However, their reign of piracy was short-lived.

In October 1720, the Governor of Jamaica, Sir Nicholas Lawes, dispatched a pirate-hunting vessel commanded by Captain Jonathan Barnet to capture Rackham and his crew. Barnet's ship caught up with Rackham's sloop near Negril, Jamaica. In the ensuing battle, Rackham's crew, reportedly drunk and unprepared, put up a feeble resistance. According to accounts, it was Bonny and Read who fought valiantly to the end, attempting to rally the drunken pirates. Despite their efforts, Rackham and his crew were captured and taken to Jamaica for trial.

The trial of Calico Jack Rackham and his crew was swift and decisive. Found guilty of piracy, they were sentenced to death. Rackham was hanged in Port Royal on November 18, 1720. His body was subsequently gibbeted—a grim post-mortem display meant to serve as a deterrent to other would-be pirates—at a place now known as Rackham's Cay. Anne Bonny and Mary Read, also captured and tried, managed to delay their executions by "pleading their bellies," a legal defense indicating they were pregnant. While Read died in prison, possibly due to complications from childbirth, Bonny's fate remains uncertain. Some accounts suggest she escaped or was released, eventually disappearing from the historical record.

Calico Jack's relatively brief career as a pirate captain belies the lasting impact of his exploits. His association with Anne Bonny and Mary Read, along with his flamboyant persona, has cemented his place in the lore of piracy. While he may not have been as successful or as feared as some of his contemporaries, the narrative of Calico Jack and his female pirates has captured the imagination of generations.

The legacy of John Rackham endures in popular culture, where he is often portrayed as a quintessential pirate—dashing, audacious, and romantically linked with fellow pirates. His life and career highlight the complexities and contradictions of the pirate world, where hierarchies could be upended, and traditional gender roles challenged. Rackham's story, intertwined with those of Anne Bonny and Mary

Read, underscores the diverse and often extraordinary lives of those who chose the perilous and unpredictable life of piracy.

In the broader context of the Golden Age of Piracy, Calico Jack represents the spirit of rebellion and adventure that characterized the era. His exploits, though not as grand as those of other pirates, illustrate the allure of the pirate life and the enduring fascination it holds. The tales of his daring raids, his dramatic capture, and the fierce women who sailed with him continue to resonate, ensuring that Calico Jack's name remains synonymous with the daring and colorful world of pirates.

Chapter 13: Bartholomew Roberts

Bartholomew Roberts, also known as Black Bart, is often regarded as one of the most successful and fearsome pirates of the Golden Age of Piracy. Born John Roberts around 1682 in Casnewydd-Bach, Pembrokeshire, Wales, he rose to prominence in a career that, though brief, left an indelible mark on the history of piracy. His real name is sometimes given as John Roberts, but he is best known by his pseudonym and the moniker "Black Bart" due to his dark hair and fearsome reputation.

Roberts' early life remains shrouded in mystery, with little documentation on his upbringing and what led him to the sea. It is believed that he went to sea at a young age, gaining experience as a mate on merchant and slaving vessels. His maritime career took a dramatic turn in 1719 when the ship he was serving on, the slaver Princess, was captured by pirates off the coast of West Africa. The pirate crew was led by Captain Howell Davis, a Welshman like Roberts. Davis recognized Roberts' navigational skills and offered him a position in his crew, a decision that would change the course of Roberts' life.

Roberts reluctantly joined the pirates, initially viewing the lifestyle with disdain. However, his attitude soon changed as he adapted to the freedom and opportunity that piracy offered. When Captain Davis was killed in an ambush by the Portuguese at Principe Island, the crew elected Roberts as their new captain. Despite his initial reluctance, Roberts accepted the role, quickly proving his mettle as a leader and strategist.

Roberts' tenure as a pirate captain was marked by audacity, tactical brilliance, and an unyielding ambition. He immediately set about avenging Davis' death by launching a successful attack on the Portuguese colony at Principe, capturing a heavily armed vessel and setting fire to the town's ships in the harbor. This act of vengeance set the tone for Roberts' piratical career, characterized by both ferocity and strategic cunning.

One of Roberts' most significant exploits occurred off the coast of Brazil in 1720. In a bold move, he sailed into the Bay of All Saints, where he discovered a fleet of 42 Portuguese merchant ships awaiting convoy protection. Despite the overwhelming odds, Roberts captured the richest ship in the fleet, the Sagrada Familia, a heavily armed vessel carrying valuable cargo. This daring raid brought Roberts immense wealth and solidified his reputation as a pirate to be reckoned with.

Roberts' success was not only due to his fearless tactics but also his ability to maintain discipline and morale among his crew. He was known for implementing a strict code of conduct, which later became famous as the "Pirate Code" or "Articles of Black Bart." This code included rules on the fair distribution of plunder, compensation for injuries, and the punishment of offenses such as theft and desertion. Roberts' ability to enforce these rules and maintain order helped him command respect and loyalty from his men, setting his leadership apart from that of many other pirate captains.

Roberts' base of operations extended across the Atlantic, from the coast of West Africa to the Caribbean and the eastern seaboard of North America. He demonstrated remarkable adaptability and strategic foresight, often evading naval patrols and shifting his operations to avoid capture. One of his most famous tactics was the use of deception and intimidation. Roberts often flew multiple flags, including those of friendly or neutral nations, to approach his targets unsuspected. His own distinctive flag, depicting a skeletal figure holding an hourglass and a spear, became a symbol of terror among merchant ships.

Roberts' exploits in the Caribbean were particularly notable. He attacked several major ports and captured numerous vessels, including the governor of Martinique's ship. In retaliation, he famously declared vengeance on the island, pledging to burn and destroy any ships from

Martinique he encountered. His raids on St. Kitts, Newfoundland, and other locations yielded significant plunder and further cemented his fearsome reputation.

Despite his successes, Roberts' career was not without its challenges and near misses. He narrowly escaped capture multiple times, often through sheer daring and clever maneuvering. His ability to inspire his crew and maintain their loyalty was crucial in these moments, allowing him to recover and continue his piratical activities. However, Roberts' luck would eventually run out.

In February 1722, Roberts was operating off the coast of West Africa, near Cape Lopez (in present-day Gabon). His fleet, now consisting of several captured ships, was intercepted by the British warship HMS Swallow, commanded by Captain Chaloner Ogle. Ogle had been specifically dispatched to hunt down and eliminate Roberts, who had become a significant threat to British shipping. In a fierce battle, the Swallow managed to outmaneuver and engage Roberts' flagship, the Royal Fortune.

During the engagement, Roberts was killed by grapeshot, a devastating blow to his crew and the pirate world at large. According to reports, Roberts had been preparing for battle, dressed in his finest clothes, as was his custom. His crew, demoralized by his death, offered little resistance, and many were captured. The captured pirates were subsequently tried and executed or imprisoned, effectively ending Roberts' reign of terror on the high seas.

Roberts' death marked the decline of the Golden Age of Piracy. His career had spanned only a few years, yet in that time, he captured an estimated 400 ships, making him one of the most successful pirates in history. His ability to combine audacity, tactical brilliance, and leadership set him apart from his contemporaries, and his impact on maritime history is profound.

The legacy of Bartholomew Roberts endures in both historical accounts and popular culture. His Pirate Code influenced subsequent generations of pirates and continues to be referenced in modern portrayals of pirate life. Roberts' life story has inspired numerous books, films, and other media, cementing his place as one of the most iconic figures in the lore of piracy.

Roberts' life and career also provide valuable insights into the socio-political context of the early 18th century. His ability to operate across vast distances and evade capture highlights the challenges faced by colonial powers in policing the high seas. The allure of piracy, with its promise of wealth and freedom, attracted individuals from diverse backgrounds, creating a complex and often unstable pirate society. Roberts' story exemplifies the dynamic interplay between authority and rebellion, order and chaos, that characterized the pirate world.

Chapter 14: Stede Bonnet

Stede Bonnet, often referred to as the "Gentleman Pirate," is a unique and intriguing figure in the annals of piracy during the Golden Age of Piracy. Born in 1688 in Bridgetown, Barbados, Bonnet's background starkly contrasts with the rough-and-tumble origins of most of his piratical peers. Hailing from a wealthy and respectable family, he inherited a sizable estate upon his father's death, which afforded him a comfortable and privileged upbringing. Bonnet's decision to turn to piracy is often attributed to a midlife crisis or dissatisfaction with his domestic life, making his story a fascinating study of a gentleman-turned-pirate.

Before embarking on his pirate career, Bonnet lived the life of a typical colonial planter. He married Mary Allamby, with whom he had three children. Despite his comfortable existence, Bonnet was reportedly unhappy in his domestic life. Some accounts suggest that marital strife and the pressures of plantation management led him to seek adventure and escape. Unlike most pirates who turned to a life of crime out of necessity or rebellion, Bonnet's entry into piracy seems to have been driven by personal discontent and a desire for excitement.

In the spring of 1717, at the age of 29, Bonnet made the extraordinary decision to become a pirate. In an unusual move for the time, he purchased a sloop named Revenge rather than capturing one. He outfitted the vessel with ten guns and hired a crew of seventy men. Bonnet's lack of maritime experience was glaring, and he relied heavily on his hired hands to navigate and conduct pirate operations. His decision to buy a ship and recruit a crew using his own wealth earned him the nickname "the Gentleman Pirate."

Bonnet's early piratical endeavors were marked by a series of misadventures and failures, highlighting his inexperience. Despite his lack of naval skills, he managed to capture several small vessels off the coast of Virginia and the Carolinas. His modus operandi typically involved boarding the captured ships and taking their cargo, often leaving the crews unharmed. However, his lack of strategic acumen and leadership soon became apparent.

In September 1717, Bonnet had a significant encounter that would shape the course of his pirate career. His ship, the Revenge, was badly damaged in a battle with a Spanish man-of-war. Seeking refuge and repairs, Bonnet sailed to Nassau, a notorious pirate haven in the Bahamas. It was here that he met Edward Teach, better known as Blackbeard. Recognizing Bonnet's ineptitude, Blackbeard took advantage of the situation. He offered Bonnet an alliance, and Bonnet, perhaps realizing his limitations as a captain, agreed.

Blackbeard effectively took command of the Revenge, relegating Bonnet to the status of a guest on his own ship. The two pirates operated together for several months, during which Blackbeard's influence and mentorship left a significant impact on Bonnet. Despite being sidelined, Bonnet observed and learned from Blackbeard's more experienced and ruthless approach to piracy. This period also saw Bonnet's capture of the Concorde, a large French ship, which was refitted and renamed the Queen Anne's Revenge by Blackbeard.

By the summer of 1718, Bonnet had regained his command, though it is unclear whether he took it back by force or if Blackbeard voluntarily relinquished control. Bonnet, now more experienced and possibly more ruthless, continued his piratical activities. However, his fortunes soon took a turn for the worse. In August 1718, Bonnet decided to seek a royal pardon, hoping to escape the life of piracy. He sailed to Bath, North Carolina, where Governor Charles Eden was known to offer pardons to repentant pirates. Bonnet received his pardon but was unable to resist the lure of the sea for long.

Bonnet's return to piracy was almost immediate. Rechristening himself as "Captain Thomas," he resumed his attacks on merchant ships along the Eastern Seaboard. However, his renewed activities quickly drew the attention of colonial authorities. In September 1718, Colonel

William Rhett, a militia officer from South Carolina, set out to capture Bonnet. Rhett's forces engaged Bonnet's ship in the Cape Fear River. After a protracted and bloody battle, Bonnet and his crew were overwhelmed and captured.

Stede Bonnet's trial took place in Charleston, South Carolina. Despite his attempts to negotiate leniency and leverage his gentlemanly status, he was found guilty of piracy. His trial attracted significant attention due to his unusual background and the notoriety he had gained during his piratical exploits. On December 10, 1718, Stede Bonnet was hanged, marking the end of his brief but colorful career as the Gentleman Pirate.

Bonnet's life as a pirate is a study in contrasts and contradictions. Unlike the typical image of a hardened, desperate buccaneer, Bonnet was a well-educated landowner who turned to piracy out of personal disillusionment. His story is marked by a series of failures and missteps, underscored by his lack of maritime skills and strategic acumen. Yet, his association with Blackbeard and his audacious decision to embrace a life of crime have cemented his place in pirate lore.

Bonnet's legacy is both fascinating and tragic. He embodies the allure of piracy during the Golden Age, a time when the line between lawful and unlawful was often blurred, and the promise of adventure and fortune drew men from all walks of life. His story also highlights the complexity of human motivation, showing how personal dissatisfaction and a desire for escape can lead to drastic and unexpected life choices.

In popular culture, Stede Bonnet has been portrayed as a somewhat comical figure, a gentleman out of his depth in the brutal world of piracy. However, this interpretation overlooks the more profound aspects of his story—his boldness in leaving behind a life of privilege, his attempts to navigate a world for which he was ill-prepared, and his ultimate downfall. His life and career offer a unique lens through which to view the broader phenomenon of piracy during the early 18th century, reflecting the era's social dynamics, economic pressures, and the enduring human quest for freedom and adventure.

Stede Bonnet's tale continues to capture the imagination of historians, writers, and enthusiasts of pirate history. His unusual path to piracy, marked by both folly and audacity, ensures that he remains one of the most memorable figures from the Golden Age of Piracy. His story is a reminder of the diverse and often surprising human stories that lie behind the romanticized image of the pirate, adding depth and nuance to our understanding of this turbulent and fascinating period in history.

Chapter 15: Charles Vane

Charles Vane is one of the most notorious pirates of the Golden Age of Piracy, a period spanning the late 17th and early 18th centuries. Born around 1680, Vane's early life is largely undocumented, with most information about him coming from his time as a pirate. His career is characterized by his fierce independence, ruthless tactics, and eventual downfall, which collectively paint a vivid picture of the chaotic and violent world of piracy during this era.

Vane first appears in historical records around 1716, operating in the Caribbean. His piratical career began under the command of Henry Jennings, another infamous pirate. Vane was part of Jennings' crew that attacked and looted the Spanish salvage camp at Palmar de Ayiz in Florida. The camp had been set up to recover treasure from the wreck of the 1715 Spanish treasure fleet, and the raid on it yielded a substantial bounty for Jennings and his men. This initial success likely whetted Vane's appetite for piracy and set the stage for his subsequent exploits.

By 1717, Vane had become a pirate captain in his own right. He operated primarily in the Bahamas, using the island of New Providence as a base. This island was a notorious pirate haven during the Golden Age, with minimal government control and a thriving community of buccaneers. Vane quickly established himself as a formidable pirate, known for his aggressive tactics and refusal to back down from a fight. His fleet grew as he captured more ships and recruited additional crew members, many of whom were drawn to his bold leadership style and reputation for success.

One of Vane's most significant and infamous encounters occurred in July 1718. The newly appointed governor of the Bahamas, Woodes Rogers, arrived in New Providence with a royal pardon for pirates willing to renounce their ways and swear allegiance to the Crown. Rogers' arrival marked a turning point in the government's efforts to suppress piracy in the region. While many pirates, including the infamous Benjamin Hornigold, accepted the pardon, Vane was staunchly opposed to it. Viewing the offer as a threat to his freedom and livelihood, Vane and his crew defiantly refused the pardon and fled New Providence.

In the weeks that followed, Vane continued his piratical activities, attacking and looting ships along the American coast. His refusal to accept the royal pardon and his continued defiance of colonial authorities earned him a reputation as one of the most uncompromising pirates of his time. Vane's fleet, which included his flagship Ranger, wreaked havoc on merchant vessels, capturing valuable cargo and evading capture through a combination of cunning and ferocity.

Vane's tactics were notoriously ruthless. Unlike some pirates who preferred to intimidate their targets into surrendering, Vane often engaged in outright combat, using superior firepower and aggressive boarding actions to overpower his enemies. His reputation for brutality spread quickly, and many merchant ships began arming themselves more heavily or traveling in convoys to avoid falling prey to Vane and his men. Despite these precautions, Vane's fleet continued to find and exploit vulnerabilities in the shipping routes of the Caribbean and North American coast.

One of the key factors in Vane's success was his ability to inspire loyalty among his crew. Unlike some pirate captains who ruled through fear or tyranny, Vane was known for his democratic approach to leadership. He adhered to the pirate code, which emphasized shared decision-making and equal distribution of plunder. This egalitarian ethos helped maintain morale and loyalty among his men, even in the face of adversity. Vane's charisma and fearless leadership style also contributed to his reputation and the effectiveness of his operations.

However, Vane's defiance and ruthlessness eventually led to conflicts within his own ranks. In November 1718, his fleet encountered a large French warship off the coast of North Carolina. Recognizing the superior firepower of the French vessel, Vane ordered a retreat. This decision was met with outrage by his crew, who viewed it as cowardly and dishonorable. The seeds of dissent had been sown, and soon after, Vane's quartermaster, "Calico" Jack Rackham, led a mutiny against him. Rackham's supporters outnumbered Vane's loyalists, and Vane was deposed and cast adrift in a small sloop with a handful of men.

Despite this setback, Vane continued his piratical activities. He managed to rebuild his crew and resume his attacks on merchant vessels. However, his fortunes took a turn for the worse in early 1719. After a series of unsuccessful engagements and dwindling resources, Vane's sloop was wrecked by a hurricane in the Bay Islands off the coast of Honduras. Vane survived the storm and washed ashore on a small, uninhabited island.

Stranded and desperate, Vane's situation grew increasingly dire. His luck finally ran out in March 1719 when he was recognized by a passing ship. Captain Holford, a former pirate who had taken the royal pardon and turned privateer, was aboard the vessel. Holford initially considered rescuing Vane but ultimately decided to leave him to his fate. Vane's reputation and ruthless past had made him too dangerous to harbor.

After several months, Vane was rescued by another vessel, but his freedom was short-lived. Upon arriving in Jamaica, Vane was recognized and arrested by colonial authorities. His trial was swift and decisive, with ample evidence of his piratical activities leading to a guilty verdict. On March 29, 1721, Charles Vane was hanged in Port Royal, Jamaica, bringing an end to his tumultuous and violent career.

Charles Vane's legacy is that of a pirate who epitomized the defiance and brutality of the Golden Age of Piracy. His refusal to accept the royal pardon and his continued attacks on shipping lanes made him a symbol of resistance against colonial authority. Vane's leadership style, which combined democratic principles with ruthless tactics, set him apart from many of his contemporaries. His story also highlights the internal conflicts and shifting allegiances that were common among pirate crews, illustrating the volatile and often short-lived nature of pirate leadership.

Vane's life and career have been the subject of numerous historical accounts, novels, and other media. His defiant stance against the colonial powers and his dramatic fall from power make him a compelling figure in the lore of piracy. While he may not have achieved the same level of infamy as some of his peers, such as Blackbeard or Captain Kidd, Vane's story remains a significant part of the broader narrative of the Golden Age of Piracy.

In the larger context of pirate history, Charles Vane represents the rebellious spirit and harsh realities of life on the high seas. His career, marked by both bold successes and ultimate failure, serves as a reminder of the perils and allure of the pirate's life. Vane's story underscores the complex motivations and personal dynamics that drove many to choose a life of piracy, reflecting the broader social and economic pressures of the time.

Ultimately, Charles Vane's legacy is one of fierce independence and unrelenting defiance. His refusal to bow to authority and his relentless pursuit of plunder, despite the risks and consequences, embody the adventurous and often perilous life of a pirate during the Golden Age. His story continues to captivate and inspire, offering a window into a world where the line between law and lawlessness was often blurred, and where the pursuit of freedom and fortune came at a high cost.

Chapter 16: Edward England

Edward England, a prominent figure in the Golden Age of Piracy, is remembered for his comparatively humane approach to piracy and his adherence to a moral code that set him apart from many of his ruthless contemporaries. Born around 1685, England's early life remains largely undocumented, with much of what is known about him coming from his years as a pirate. His career, marked by notable successes and eventual betrayal, provides a fascinating glimpse into the complex social dynamics and operational methods of pirate crews during this tumultuous period.

Edward England's piratical career began in earnest in the early 18th century, likely around 1717 or 1718. Before turning to piracy, it is believed that he served as a privateer during the War of the Spanish Succession, a common precursor to piracy for many men of the sea during this era. Privateers were authorized by governments to attack enemy ships, and the transition from privateering to piracy was a natural one for those who found themselves out of work or disillusioned at the war's end.

England's first documented foray into piracy occurred while he was serving on a Jamaican sloop under the command of a captain named Winter. After capturing a vessel off the coast of Africa, the crew mutinied, and England was elected as their leader. His election as captain reflected the democratic practices common among pirate crews, who valued leadership skills and shared decision-making over rigid hierarchies.

Under England's command, the crew captured several ships, gradually increasing their strength and reputation. His early successes included the capture of the Cadogan, an English vessel whose crew was coerced into joining the pirates. The Cadogan was later sold in Africa, and England continued to expand his operations. His humane treatment of prisoners and adherence to a code of conduct began to distinguish him from other pirate captains known for their brutality and lack of restraint.

One of England's most notable captures was the Pearl, a large slave ship taken off the coast of West Africa. The Pearl was armed and renamed the Royal James, becoming one of the most formidable ships in England's fleet. This acquisition marked a significant escalation in England's piratical capabilities, allowing him to take on more ambitious targets and venture further afield.

England's base of operations extended from the coast of West Africa to the Indian Ocean, a region teeming with lucrative targets, including merchant vessels from the East India Company. In 1719, England's fleet sailed to Madagascar, a well-known pirate haven. There, they joined forces with other notorious pirates, such as Christopher Condent and John Taylor, forming a formidable coalition that posed a significant threat to maritime trade in the Indian Ocean.

One of the most famous exploits of England's career occurred in 1720 when he captured the Cassandra, a heavily armed East Indiaman commanded by Captain James Macrae. The battle was fierce, with England's flagship, the Fancy, sustaining heavy damage. Despite being outgunned, England's crew managed to board and capture the Cassandra after a protracted and bloody fight. England's treatment of Macrae and his crew after the battle was a testament to his relatively humane approach to piracy. Instead of executing them or subjecting them to brutal conditions, England provided Macrae with a ship, supplies, and safe passage, a decision that later earned him both admiration and criticism from his peers.

The capture of the Cassandra was a significant victory for England, but it also marked the beginning of his downfall. Dissatisfaction and dissent began to brew among his crew, who viewed his lenient treatment of Macrae as a sign of weakness. The pirate code, while emphasizing fairness and shared decision-making, also demanded decisive and often ruthless action against enemies. England's principles, which set him apart from more bloodthirsty captains, ultimately contributed to his undoing.

In the aftermath of the Cassandra capture, England's crew deposed him in a mutiny led by his quartermaster, John Taylor. Taylor, representing the more ruthless faction of the crew, seized command and marooned England and a few loyalists on the island of Mauritius. Stranded and abandoned, England's situation grew increasingly dire. Despite the hostile environment, he managed to survive for some time, eking out a precarious existence with limited resources.

Edward England's life came to a tragic end in 1721. According to most accounts, he died in poverty and despair, a stark contrast to the power and influence he wielded during his peak as a pirate captain. His death marked the conclusion of a career that, while shorter and less violent than those of many of his contemporaries, left a lasting legacy in the annals of pirate history.

England's story is significant not only for his achievements but also for his approach to piracy. In an era characterized by ruthless violence and cruelty, his relatively humane treatment of prisoners and adherence to a code of conduct provide a unique perspective on the pirate lifestyle. His leadership style, which balanced authority with fairness, highlights the complex social dynamics within pirate crews and the often precarious nature of their alliances.

The legacy of Edward England endures in both historical records and popular culture. He is remembered as a pirate who, despite operating within a lawless and brutal world, maintained a sense of moral integrity and humanity. His story has been the subject of numerous books, films, and other media, reflecting the enduring fascination with the Golden Age of Piracy and its colorful characters.

England's life also offers insights into the broader context of piracy during the early 18th century. The economic and social conditions that drove men to piracy, the democratic structures within pirate crews, and the constant tension between cooperation and conflict are all reflected in his career. His interactions with other pirates, colonial authorities, and merchant captains reveal the complex web of relationships that defined the pirate world.

Chapter 17: John Quelch

John Quelch was an English pirate whose career, though brief, was marked by bold exploits and a dramatic downfall. Born around 1666, Quelch's early life remains largely undocumented, with much of what is known about him coming from his final years as a pirate. His story provides a fascinating glimpse into the complexities of piracy, colonial politics, and maritime law during the early 18th century.

Quelch's transition to piracy began against a backdrop of political and economic turbulence. The War of Spanish Succession (1701-1714) created opportunities for privateers, who were authorized by their governments to attack enemy ships. However, the line between privateering and piracy was often thin, and many privateers turned to outright piracy, either out of greed or necessity. Quelch was among those who seized the opportunity to embark on a life of piracy.

In 1703, Quelch was serving as the first mate on the Charles, a brigantine commissioned as a privateer by Governor Joseph Dudley of the Province of Massachusetts Bay. The Charles was tasked with patrolling the New England coast and the Caribbean, targeting French and Spanish vessels. However, the mission took an unexpected turn when Captain Daniel Plowman fell ill. Quelch and a faction of the crew seized this moment to stage a mutiny. Plowman was either murdered or left to die, and Quelch assumed command of the vessel.

Under Quelch's leadership, the Charles deviated from its privateering mission. Instead of pursuing French and Spanish targets in the Caribbean, Quelch led the ship across the Atlantic to the coast of Brazil, then a Portuguese territory. This move was highly significant because Portugal was an ally of England in the War of Spanish Succession. By attacking Portuguese ships, Quelch and his crew were committing acts of piracy against a friendly nation, which would later have severe legal repercussions.

Quelch's exploits off the coast of Brazil were marked by significant success. The Charles captured several Portuguese ships laden with valuable cargo, including gold dust, sugar, and hides. These prizes promised immense wealth for Quelch and his crew. The most notable of these captures was the Portuguese ship known as the "New Sloop," which was carrying a substantial amount of gold dust. The riches obtained from these raids fueled both the greed and the boldness of Quelch's crew, but they also set the stage for their eventual downfall.

After amassing their ill-gotten gains, Quelch and his crew sailed back to New England in the spring of 1704. They landed on the coast of Marblehead, Massachusetts, where they attempted to discreetly divide and dispose of their loot. However, the sudden influx of gold and valuable goods quickly aroused suspicion among the local authorities and merchants. News of Quelch's activities soon reached Boston, where Governor Dudley, keen to uphold colonial law and maintain relations with Portugal, took swift action.

Governor Dudley ordered the arrest of Quelch and his crew, who were charged with piracy against the Portuguese, an ally of England. The trial of John Quelch and his men was notable for several reasons. It was one of the first piracy trials held in the American colonies under the Admiralty law, which allowed for the prosecution of pirates in colonial courts. The trial was conducted with great fanfare and public interest, underscoring the colonial authorities' determination to make an example of Quelch.

During the trial, Quelch and his men were charged with piracy and murder. The evidence against them was overwhelming, including testimonies from crew members who had turned against their captain in hopes of leniency. Quelch attempted to argue that his actions were legitimate acts of privateering, but the court rejected this defense, emphasizing that Portugal was an ally, not an enemy. The jury found Quelch and several of his crew members guilty, and they were sentenced to death.

John Quelch's execution on June 30, 1704, was a dramatic and public affair. He and six of his men were hanged at Nix's Mate, a small island in Boston Harbor that was traditionally used for the execution of pirates. Quelch's last words were reported to be a warning to the spectators: "They should take care how they brought money into New England, to be hanged for it." This statement highlighted the complex and often contradictory nature of colonial attitudes towards piracy and wealth.

Quelch's story did not end with his death. His trial and execution had significant implications for the colonial legal system and the prosecution of piracy. The trial was one of the first to be conducted under the Admiralty law in the American colonies, setting a precedent for future cases. It also underscored the shifting attitudes towards piracy as colonial authorities sought to assert greater control over their territories and maintain diplomatic relations with European powers.

Quelch's life and career have since become the subject of historical interest and folklore. His exploits, trial, and dramatic execution provide a window into the world of early 18th-century piracy, colonial politics, and maritime law. Quelch's decision to turn to piracy, his daring raids off the coast of Brazil, and his ultimate downfall illustrate the precarious nature of a pirate's life and the fine line between privateering and piracy.

In the larger context of pirate history, John Quelch's story is significant for several reasons. First, it highlights the role of privateering as a precursor to piracy, showing how economic opportunities and political conflicts could drive men to the edge of the law. Second, it illustrates the complexities of colonial law and the efforts of colonial authorities to control and punish piracy. Finally, it offers a glimpse into the social dynamics of pirate crews, including the motivations, loyalties, and betrayals that shaped their actions.

Quelch's relatively brief career as a pirate is a testament to the volatility and danger of the piratical life. His bold decision to raid

Portuguese ships, driven by the lure of immense wealth, ultimately led to his capture and execution. His story is a reminder of the high stakes and fleeting nature of success in the world of piracy, where fortune and death often went hand in hand.

Chapter 18: William Fly

William Fly was an infamous pirate whose brief but bloody career on the high seas left a lasting impression on maritime history. Born around 1664, Fly's early life remains shrouded in mystery, with little known about his upbringing or how he initially became involved in seafaring. His life as a pirate, however, is better documented, particularly the dramatic and violent events that led to his capture and execution in 1726.

Fly's piracy career began as a crew member aboard the slave ship, the Elizabeth, under the command of Captain John Green. The conditions aboard the ship were harsh, with the crew facing brutal treatment, inadequate rations, and a tyrannical captain. The mutinous sentiments among the crew reached a boiling point when they decided to take matters into their own hands. On April 27, 1726, Fly led a mutiny against Captain Green, a decisive and violent uprising that ended with Green's murder. Fly and his cohorts seized control of the vessel, rechristening it the Fames' Revenge, and set sail as pirates.

The newly formed pirate crew quickly embarked on a spree of piracy along the American coast and the Caribbean. Fly proved to be a ruthless and efficient leader, instilling fear both in his enemies and within his crew. His tactics were brutal, often employing violence and intimidation to subdue targets. Under his command, the crew captured several ships, plundering their cargo and wealth. Despite his ruthless efficiency, Fly's reign as a pirate captain was marked by a lack of discipline and organization, which would eventually contribute to his downfall.

One notable incident in Fly's brief piratical career involved the capture of the sloop John and Hannah off the coast of Massachusetts. After taking control of the sloop, Fly and his men subjected its captain, John Gale, and the crew to a harsh ordeal. Fly's propensity for violence and cruelty was evident as he tormented his captives, leaving a trail of fear and animosity in his wake. Such incidents contributed to the growing determination among colonial authorities and merchants to bring an end to Fly's depredations.

The turning point came in June 1726, when Fly and his crew captured another vessel near the Massachusetts coast. The Fames' Revenge, now infamous and highly recognizable, was sighted by a group of determined bounty hunters led by the resourceful Captain Peter Solgard. Solgard, commanding the HMS Greyhound, pursued Fly's ship with relentless vigor. After a fierce and desperate battle, Solgard succeeded in capturing Fly and his remaining crew. The engagement was a significant triumph for Solgard and a stark illustration of the growing capabilities of colonial anti-piracy efforts.

Fly and his men were transported to Boston, where they were swiftly tried for piracy. The trial was a spectacle, drawing considerable public attention. Fly, defiant and unrepentant, used the proceedings to voice his grievances against the harsh treatment of sailors by their captains. He maintained that his actions were in retaliation against the abuses he and his fellow seamen had suffered. Despite his protestations, the court found him guilty of piracy.

On July 12, 1726, William Fly was hanged at Boston's Execution Dock, alongside three of his crew members. His execution was intended not only as a punishment but also as a grim warning to others who might consider taking up the pirate's trade. Fly's last moments were marked by his refusal to repent and his scornful attitude towards his executioners. He reportedly tied his own noose, demonstrating a final act of defiance. His body was left hanging in a gibbet as a deterrent to would-be pirates.

The legacy of William Fly is multifaceted. On one hand, he is remembered as a brutal and notorious pirate whose actions contributed to the perilous reputation of pirates in the early 18th century. His career exemplified the lawlessness and violence that characterized the Golden Age of Piracy. On the other hand, Fly's outspoken criticisms of the treatment of sailors shed light on the harsh conditions and abuses that many seamen faced, highlighting the systemic issues within the maritime industry of the time.

Fly's life and death underscore the complex and often contradictory nature of piracy. While he was undoubtedly a criminal, his motivations and actions also reflected broader social and economic grievances. His story serves as a reminder of the thin line between villainy and victimhood, and the ways in which desperation and brutality can arise from oppression and mistreatment.

In the annals of piracy, William Fly's career was brief but impactful. His rise from mutinous sailor to feared pirate captain, and his subsequent capture and execution, illustrate the volatile and perilous nature of life on the high seas during the Golden Age of Piracy. His story is a testament to the harsh realities faced by sailors of the era and the extreme measures some took in response to those conditions. Though his name may not be as widely recognized as some of his contemporaries, Fly's legacy endures as a vivid example of the enduring human struggle against injustice and the lengths to which individuals will go to assert their autonomy in the face of oppression.

Chapter 19: Charlotte de Berry

Charlotte de Berry, an enigmatic figure from the 17th century, is often celebrated in the annals of pirate lore as one of the few notable female pirates. Her story, blending elements of myth and reality, paints a picture of a woman who defied the rigid gender norms of her time, taking to the seas in pursuit of freedom and revenge. Although the historical accuracy of her tale is debated, the legend of Charlotte de Berry has captivated imaginations for centuries, inspiring numerous retellings in literature and popular culture.

According to the most widely accepted version of her story, Charlotte de Berry was born in England around the early 1600s. From a young age, she exhibited a strong-willed and adventurous spirit. As a teenager, she fell in love with a sailor, a passion that set the course for her tumultuous life. Her parents, disapproving of her relationship, tried to arrange a marriage with a suitor of their choice. In defiance, Charlotte eloped with her sailor lover, disguising herself as a man to join him aboard his ship. For some time, she served alongside him, maintaining her disguise and gaining valuable seafaring skills.

The couple's happiness was short-lived. When Charlotte's true identity was discovered, her lover was accused of insubordination and sentenced to death. Consumed by grief and rage, Charlotte vowed revenge against those who had wronged her. Her transformation from a grieving widow to a fierce pirate is where legend and fact begin to intertwine.

Charlotte's vengeance began with her taking command of a ship, leading a mutiny against a tyrannical captain. She and her loyal followers seized control, and Charlotte declared herself captain. Under her leadership, the crew embarked on a series of daring raids along the African coast and the Atlantic. Charlotte's reputation grew as a fierce and cunning pirate, unmatched in her strategic acumen and fearlessness. She dressed as a man to command respect and authority, yet her true identity became known among her crew, who admired and feared her in equal measure.

One of the most dramatic episodes in Charlotte de Berry's legend involves her capture by a notorious pirate hunter. After a fierce battle, she was overpowered and taken prisoner. Imprisoned on a slave ship bound for the Caribbean, Charlotte endured harsh conditions and brutal treatment. However, her indomitable spirit and leadership qualities rallied the other prisoners. Together, they staged a rebellion, seizing control of the ship and turning it into a pirate vessel under Charlotte's command. This event solidified her status as a legendary pirate captain, one who could not be subdued or defeated easily.

Charlotte's piratical career was marked by numerous encounters with other pirates and naval forces. She forged alliances with other pirate captains, often commanding a small fleet of ships. Her strategic prowess and daring tactics allowed her to outmaneuver and outfight many of her adversaries. Despite the inherent dangers of her lifestyle, she maintained a strict code of conduct among her crew, enforcing discipline and loyalty.

The final chapter of Charlotte de Berry's story varies depending on the source. One popular version tells of her tragic end, where she and her crew were shipwrecked on the African coast. Stranded and facing starvation, the crew turned to cannibalism, with Charlotte being among the last to perish. Another account suggests that she retired from piracy, having amassed a considerable fortune, and lived out her days in anonymity.

Despite the lack of concrete historical evidence, the legend of Charlotte de Berry endures as a powerful narrative of defiance and resilience. Her story challenges the traditional perceptions of women's roles in the 17th century, presenting a figure who broke free from societal constraints to carve out her destiny on the high seas. The scarcity of records about her life adds to the mystique, allowing her legend to grow and adapt over time.

Charlotte de Berry's legacy can be seen in various cultural references, from literature to film. Her story has inspired countless fictional adaptations, each adding new dimensions to her character and exploits. She stands as a symbol of rebellion against oppression, embodying the spirit of adventure and the quest for justice. Whether entirely factual or largely fictional, the tale of Charlotte de Berry continues to resonate, reminding us of the enduring power of myth and the timeless appeal of a life lived on one's own terms.

In examining the legend of Charlotte de Berry, it is essential to recognize the broader context of female piracy in history. While women pirates were rare, they were not entirely absent. Figures like Anne Bonny and Mary Read, who operated during the Golden Age of Piracy in the early 18th century, provide historical parallels to Charlotte's story. These women, like Charlotte, defied gender norms and societal expectations, taking on leadership roles in the male-dominated world of piracy.

The romanticized image of Charlotte de Berry, as with many pirate legends, often glosses over the harsh realities of piracy. The life of a pirate was fraught with danger, brutality, and uncertainty. For many, it was a last resort, driven by desperation and a desire for freedom from oppressive circumstances. Charlotte's story, though embellished, captures these themes, offering a narrative of empowerment and resistance.

Chapter 20: Jean Thomas Dulaien

Jean Thomas Dulaien, a pirate from the 17th century, remains a shadowy yet captivating figure in the annals of maritime history. Much of his life and exploits have been obscured by time, with various sources offering fragmented accounts that blend fact and legend. Nonetheless, the story of Dulaien, as pieced together from historical records and folklore, presents a vivid picture of a man who embraced the perilous life of a pirate, navigating the treacherous waters of the Atlantic and Caribbean during a time when piracy was rampant.

Jean Thomas Dulaien was born in the early 17th century, although the exact date and location of his birth remain unknown. Some accounts suggest he hailed from France, a nation with a long history of seafaring and privateering. His early life is shrouded in mystery, but it is likely that he grew up near the coast, exposed to the maritime traditions that would later define his life. The tumultuous political and economic conditions of 17th-century Europe, marked by wars, trade rivalries, and colonial expansion, created a fertile ground for piracy. Many young men, driven by poverty, adventure, or the promise of wealth, took to the seas, and Dulaien was no exception.

Dulaien's entry into piracy was likely influenced by the chaotic maritime environment of his time. The decline of Spanish dominance in the New World and the rise of other European powers, such as England, France, and the Netherlands, led to increased naval conflicts and opportunities for privateers and pirates. It is believed that Dulaien initially served as a privateer, legally sanctioned by his government to attack enemy ships and disrupt their trade. Privateering was a common practice, blurring the lines between lawful privateers and outright pirates.

At some point, Dulaien transitioned from privateering to piracy, possibly due to the allure of greater autonomy and profit. Unlike privateers, who operated under letters of marque, pirates answered to no one but themselves, making their own rules and keeping all the spoils. This shift marked the beginning of Dulaien's notorious career as a pirate. He assembled a crew of like-minded individuals, men who were willing to risk their lives for the promise of fortune and freedom.

Dulaien and his crew operated primarily in the Atlantic Ocean and the Caribbean Sea, regions teeming with lucrative targets. The Caribbean, in particular, was a hotspot for piracy, with its numerous islands, hidden coves, and busy shipping lanes. Spanish galleons laden with gold and silver from the New World, as well as merchant ships carrying goods between Europe, Africa, and the Americas, were prime targets for pirates like Dulaien.

One of the most famous episodes in Dulaien's piratical career was his attack on a Spanish treasure fleet. The fleet, heavily guarded and transporting a vast amount of wealth, was considered a formidable challenge even for the most daring pirates. Dulaien, however, saw it as an opportunity too great to pass up. He meticulously planned the assault, taking advantage of his knowledge of the sea and the weaknesses of his adversaries. The attack was swift and brutal, resulting in a significant haul of treasure for Dulaien and his crew. This victory not only enriched them but also elevated Dulaien's status among his peers, earning him a fearsome reputation.

Dulaien's success as a pirate was not without its challenges. The colonial powers of the time were increasingly determined to stamp out piracy, which threatened their economic interests and maritime security. Navies were dispatched to hunt down pirate ships, and lucrative bounties were offered for the capture of notorious pirates. Dulaien, aware of the growing dangers, employed various tactics to evade capture. He utilized the natural geography of the Caribbean, hiding in secluded bays and navigating treacherous waters that were difficult for larger naval ships to traverse. His intimate knowledge of the region gave him an advantage, allowing him to strike swiftly and disappear before reinforcements could arrive.

Despite his cunning and resourcefulness, Dulaien's luck eventually ran out. The details of his capture are varied, with some accounts suggesting he was betrayed by a member of his crew, while others claim he was cornered by a naval squadron during a fierce battle. Regardless of how it happened, Dulaien was captured and brought to trial. His trial, like those of many pirates, was a public spectacle, drawing large crowds eager to see the infamous pirate brought to justice. He was found guilty of piracy, and his execution was meant to serve as a warning to others who might consider taking up the pirate's trade.

Jean Thomas Dulaien's execution marked the end of his life but not the end of his legacy. His exploits continued to be recounted in seafaring tales and pirate lore, contributing to the romanticized image of the swashbuckling pirate. Dulaien's story, like those of many pirates, straddles the line between history and legend, with the paucity of reliable records allowing for embellishment and myth-making.

The legacy of Jean Thomas Dulaien is a testament to the complex nature of piracy in the 17th century. Pirates were both feared and admired, seen as ruthless criminals by the authorities and as daring adventurers by the public. They lived in a world where the boundaries between legality and illegality were often blurred, and where the promise of freedom and wealth could drive men to extraordinary lengths.

In the broader context of maritime history, Dulaien's story highlights the socio-economic conditions that gave rise to piracy. The 17th century was a time of significant upheaval, with the expansion of European empires, the transatlantic slave trade, and the exploitation of New World resources creating vast inequalities and opportunities for rebellion. Pirates like Dulaien exploited these conditions, challenging the established order and carving out their own destinies on the high seas.

Dulaien's legacy also underscores the role of narrative in shaping historical memory. The stories of pirates, often embellished and romanticized, reflect societal attitudes and values. They serve as cautionary tales, moral lessons, and sources of entertainment. The enduring fascination with pirates speaks to a human desire for adventure, rebellion, and the breaking of societal constraints.

Chapter 21: Bartolomeu Português

Bartolomeu Português, a pirate of Portuguese origin, was one of the most notorious buccaneers of the 17th century. Operating primarily in the Caribbean and along the Spanish Main, he played a significant role during the Golden Age of Piracy. His career, marked by daring exploits and extraordinary escapes, has earned him a place in the annals of pirate history.

Born around the early 17th century, Bartolomeu Português's early life remains largely undocumented. However, it is speculated that he was born in Portugal, a country with a rich maritime tradition. Like many of his contemporaries, he may have been driven to piracy by the harsh economic conditions of the time, the allure of wealth, and the spirit of adventure. The Caribbean and the Spanish Main were hotbeds of pirate activity during this period, offering ample opportunities for those willing to risk their lives for fortune.

Bartolomeu Português first emerges in historical records in the mid-1660s. He quickly gained a reputation for his boldness and tactical acumen. One of his earliest and most famous exploits was the capture of a large Spanish galleon off the coast of Cuba. The galleon, heavily laden with valuable cargo including gold, silver, and other precious goods, was a formidable prize. Bartolomeu and his men, operating from smaller, faster vessels, executed a surprise attack, overwhelming the Spanish crew and seizing the ship.

The capture of the galleon was a significant coup, but it also brought immediate challenges. Knowing that Spanish authorities would pursue him relentlessly, Bartolomeu devised a daring plan to evade capture. He ordered his men to take the galleon into the mouth of a river, where they transferred the loot to their smaller ships, capable of navigating the shallow waters and dense mangroves. This maneuver allowed them to disappear into the labyrinthine waterways, evading the Spanish fleet sent to recapture the prize.

Bartolomeu's ingenuity and knowledge of the local geography were crucial to his success as a pirate. He often utilized the intricate network of rivers and islands in the Caribbean to his advantage, staging ambushes and hiding from pursuing naval forces. His ability to think quickly and adapt to changing circumstances earned him the respect of his crew and the fear of his enemies.

Despite his successes, Bartolomeu's career was fraught with peril. One of the most dramatic episodes of his life occurred when he was captured by the Spanish and imprisoned in Havana. Facing execution, he managed a remarkable escape, reportedly bribing his guards and swimming across the bay to freedom. This feat only added to his legend, demonstrating his unyielding determination and resourcefulness.

Upon his escape, Bartolomeu returned to piracy with renewed vigor. He continued to target Spanish ships and settlements, amassing considerable wealth and solidifying his reputation as one of the most formidable pirates of his time. His tactics often involved surprising his enemies with sudden and ferocious attacks, leveraging the element of surprise to his advantage.

Bartolomeu's operations were not limited to the high seas. He also conducted raids on coastal settlements, exploiting the often-limited defenses of these communities. His raids were characterized by their swiftness and brutality, designed to instill fear and secure quick capitulations. The wealth he accumulated from these ventures was significant, though it came at great risk.

The Golden Age of Piracy, during which Bartolomeu operated, was a period marked by significant geopolitical and economic upheaval. European powers were vying for control of the New World, with vast resources at stake. This competition created an environment in which piracy could flourish, as privateers and pirates alike sought to exploit the chaos and enrich themselves. Bartolomeu, like many pirates of his era, was a product of this turbulent time, driven by both personal ambition and the broader currents of history.

One of the key aspects of Bartolomeu's career was his ability to form alliances with other pirates. The loosely organized but formidable buccaneer communities of the Caribbean often cooperated to launch large-scale attacks against heavily defended targets. These alliances were pragmatic, based on mutual benefit and shared risk. Bartolomeu's leadership and reputation made him a valuable ally in these ventures, and he participated in several notable joint operations.

Despite his success, Bartolomeu's career was marked by constant danger and the ever-present threat of capture or death. The Spanish authorities, in particular, were relentless in their efforts to capture him, viewing him as a significant threat to their maritime dominance. Bartolomeu's ability to evade capture for so long is a testament to his skill as a navigator and his understanding of the treacherous waters of the Caribbean.

Bartolomeu's legacy is one of audacity and tactical brilliance. His exploits have been immortalized in various accounts of pirate history, highlighting his ability to outmaneuver more powerful adversaries and his unbreakable spirit. His story, like those of many pirates, is a mix of documented fact and legend, contributing to the romanticized image of the swashbuckling buccaneer.

The capture and daring escape from Havana, in particular, stand out as defining moments in Bartolomeu's career. These events underscore the perilous nature of piracy and the lengths to which pirates would go to secure their freedom and continue their pursuit of wealth. Bartolomeu's ability to navigate these challenges speaks to his resilience and cunning, qualities that were essential for survival in the cutthroat world of 17th-century piracy.

In the broader context of pirate history, Bartolomeu Português represents the quintessential pirate archetype: bold, resourceful, and unyielding in the face of adversity. His life and exploits provide a window into the turbulent world of the Caribbean during the Golden Age of Piracy, a time when the seas were a battleground for control and riches. Bartolomeu's story, though perhaps not as widely known as those of some other pirates, remains a compelling chapter in the rich tapestry of maritime history.

Bartolomeu Português's impact on the history of piracy extends beyond his individual achievements. He was part of a larger movement of buccaneers and privateers who challenged the established powers of the time, carving out their own destinies in defiance of the laws and conventions of their day. His career exemplifies the complex interplay between legality and outlawry, as many pirates began their careers as privateers before turning to outright piracy.

The legacy of Bartolomeu Português, like that of many pirates, is one of both historical significance and cultural fascination. Pirates have long captured the popular imagination, symbolizing both the allure of adventure and the dangers of lawlessness. Bartolomeu's story contributes to this enduring fascination, offering a narrative of courage, ingenuity, and the relentless pursuit of freedom and fortune.

Chapter 22: Emanuel Wynn

Emanuel Wynn, a pirate who operated primarily in the early 1700s, is remembered as one of the first to fly the iconic Jolly Roger flag, symbolizing the Golden Age of Piracy. His career, though not as extensively documented as those of some of his contemporaries, provides significant insights into the life and tactics of early 18th-century pirates. Wynn's actions, strategies, and the legends that surround him contribute to the rich tapestry of pirate history.

Emanuel Wynn's origins remain largely obscure, with little known about his early life or how he came to be involved in piracy. It is speculated that he may have been of French origin, as records indicate his operations were primarily off the coast of the Bahamas and the Carolinas, regions frequented by French privateers and pirates. The early 18th century was a time of intense maritime activity, with many seafarers turning to piracy due to the economic opportunities it presented amid the chaos of European conflicts and colonial expansion.

Wynn first appears in historical records in 1700, operating in the Caribbean Sea, a hotbed for pirate activity. The Caribbean's numerous islands, secluded coves, and busy shipping lanes made it an ideal region for pirates to launch their attacks and evade capture. Wynn quickly established himself as a formidable presence in these waters, known for his strategic acumen and ruthless efficiency.

One of Wynn's most notable contributions to pirate lore was his use of the Jolly Roger flag. While pirates had long used various flags to intimidate their enemies, Wynn is often credited as the first to use the classic skull and crossbones design that became synonymous with piracy. This flag served not only as a symbol of terror but also as a psychological weapon. It signaled to potential victims that resistance would be met with deadly force, often prompting them to surrender without a fight. The Jolly Roger thus became an essential tool in a pirate's arsenal, embodying the fearsome reputation that Wynn and his fellow pirates cultivated.

Wynn's career was marked by several notable engagements with merchant and naval ships. His tactics typically involved swift, surprise attacks that left little time for his targets to mount a defense. He preferred to operate in smaller, faster vessels that could easily outmaneuver larger, more cumbersome ships. This approach allowed him to strike quickly and retreat before reinforcements could arrive, minimizing the risk of capture.

One of the most significant encounters in Wynn's career was his clash with HMS Poole, a British warship commanded by Captain John Cranby. This engagement occurred near the coast of Cape Verde, a strategic location for pirates due to its position along major shipping routes. Wynn's ship, armed with numerous cannons and manned by a seasoned crew, engaged in a fierce battle with HMS Poole. Despite being outgunned, Wynn's tactical expertise allowed him to inflict substantial damage on the British ship. The battle ended inconclusively, with Wynn managing to escape into the open sea. This encounter showcased Wynn's ability to hold his own against formidable naval forces, further enhancing his reputation.

Wynn's success as a pirate was not solely due to his martial prowess. He was also known for his ability to forge alliances with other pirates and privateers. These alliances allowed him to undertake larger and more ambitious raids, pooling resources and manpower to target heavily defended merchant convoys and coastal settlements. The collaborative nature of these operations exemplified the loose but effective networks that pirates often formed, based on mutual benefit and shared risk.

Despite his successes, Wynn's career was fraught with danger. The increasing efforts of colonial powers to suppress piracy meant that he was constantly pursued by naval patrols and bounty hunters. The growing naval presence in the Caribbean and Atlantic made it increasingly difficult for pirates to operate with impunity. Wynn's ability to evade capture for so long is a testament to his cunning and adaptability.

The exact details of Emanuel Wynn's fate remain unclear, with various accounts suggesting different outcomes. Some sources claim that he was eventually captured and executed by the British, while others suggest he may have retired from piracy and disappeared into obscurity. The lack of concrete records makes it difficult to ascertain the true end of his story, adding an element of mystery to his legend.

Wynn's legacy, however, is more enduring than his individual exploits. He played a pivotal role in shaping the iconography and tactics of piracy during the early 18th century. The use of the Jolly Roger flag, in particular, became a defining symbol of pirate identity, adopted by many other pirates in the years that followed. This flag, with its stark imagery of death, encapsulated the fearsome reputation that pirates sought to project, and its origins are closely associated with Wynn's career.

The era in which Wynn operated, known as the Golden Age of Piracy, was a period marked by significant geopolitical and economic shifts. The decline of Spanish dominance in the New World, the rise of British and French colonial ambitions, and the vast wealth flowing from the Americas created a volatile environment ripe for piracy. Pirates like Wynn thrived in this context, exploiting the chaos and asserting their own form of maritime rebellion.

Wynn's story, though less well-documented than those of pirates like Blackbeard or Bartholomew Roberts, offers valuable insights into the operational strategies and symbolic tactics that defined early 18th-century piracy. His use of the Jolly Roger, his ability to outmaneuver superior naval forces, and his alliances with other pirates exemplify the blend of terror, cunning, and collaboration that characterized the pirate's life.

In the broader cultural memory, Wynn's legacy contributes to the romanticized image of the pirate as a figure of defiance and adventure. The enduring fascination with pirates, fueled by literature, film, and folklore, often glosses over the brutal realities of piracy, focusing instead on the daring exploits and rebellious spirit that figures like Wynn embodied. This romanticized view, while not entirely accurate, underscores the powerful hold that pirate legends have on the popular imagination.

Chapter 23: Anne Bonny

Anne Bonny, one of the most notorious female pirates of the early 18th century, remains a captivating figure in the annals of piracy. Her life story, filled with adventure, defiance, and intrigue, offers a unique glimpse into the world of piracy during its Golden Age. Born around 1700 and living until approximately 1782, Anne Bonny's tale is a blend of documented history and legend, contributing to her enduring legacy as a symbol of female rebellion and maritime audacity.

Anne Bonny was born Anne Cormac around 1700 in County Cork, Ireland. Her father, William Cormac, was a successful lawyer, and her mother, Mary Brennan, was a servant. The circumstances of Anne's birth were scandalous, as her father had an extramarital affair with Mary, which led to her parents fleeing to the American colonies to avoid the ensuing social disgrace. They settled in Charles Town (now Charleston), South Carolina, where her father established himself as a prosperous merchant.

Growing up in the bustling port town of Charles Town, Anne was exposed to the maritime culture that dominated the region. She developed a strong-willed and adventurous personality, often rebelling against the conventional expectations placed on women of her time. By her teenage years, Anne had earned a reputation for her fiery temper and indomitable spirit. One famous story from her youth recounts how she supposedly stabbed a servant girl with a knife, showcasing her fierce nature.

Anne's rebellious streak extended to her personal life. At around sixteen, she married James Bonny, a small-time pirate and sailor, against her father's wishes. This marriage further alienated her from her family, leading to a final break with her father. The couple moved to Nassau in the Bahamas, a haven for pirates and privateers, where James hoped to capitalize on the thriving pirate economy. Nassau, known as the

"Republic of Pirates," was a hotbed of pirate activity, offering sanctuary and a vibrant community for outlaws.

It was in Nassau that Anne's life took a dramatic turn. Disenchanted with her husband, who reportedly became an informant for the Governor of the Bahamas, Anne sought out the company of more daring and influential pirates. It was during this time that she met and fell in love with the infamous pirate captain John "Calico Jack" Rackham. Rackham, known for his distinctive calico clothing, was a charismatic and successful pirate who commanded a loyal crew.

Anne Bonny and Calico Jack began a passionate and tumultuous relationship. Anne joined Rackham's crew, disguising herself as a man to avoid the stigma and danger associated with women on pirate ships. Her disguise allowed her to participate fully in the crew's activities, including combat and plundering, without drawing undue attention. However, it is believed that Rackham and many of the crew knew her true identity and respected her for her bravery and skill.

Anne quickly proved herself to be a formidable pirate. She was known for her fierce fighting abilities, wielding a cutlass and pistols with deadly efficiency. Her participation in boarding enemy ships and leading raids alongside the male pirates earned her a reputation as a fierce and fearless combatant. Anne's boldness and leadership qualities made her an integral part of Rackham's crew, challenging the conventional gender roles of her time.

During her time with Rackham, Anne formed a close bond with another female pirate, Mary Read. Read, like Anne, had disguised herself as a man to join the pirate life. The two women became fast friends, supporting each other in the male-dominated world of piracy. Their camaraderie and mutual respect were pivotal in their survival and success. The presence of two female pirates on Rackham's ship was highly unusual and contributed to the legendary status of their crew.

Rackham, Bonny, and Read embarked on a series of daring raids across the Caribbean, targeting merchant ships and coastal settlements.

They operated with a mix of audacity and cunning, often employing surprise attacks to overwhelm their adversaries. Their exploits brought them considerable wealth and notoriety, but also attracted the attention of colonial authorities determined to stamp out piracy.

In October 1720, their luck ran out. Rackham's ship was anchored off the coast of Jamaica when they were surprised by a British naval sloop commanded by Captain Jonathan Barnet. Rackham and his crew were caught off guard, many of them too drunk to mount an effective defense. Anne Bonny and Mary Read, however, fought fiercely, reportedly holding off Barnet's men for some time before being overpowered. Their resistance was noted by witnesses, further cementing their reputation as fearsome pirates.

The captured pirates were taken to Spanish Town, Jamaica, where they were put on trial for piracy. Rackham and his male crew were swiftly convicted and sentenced to hang. Anne and Mary, however, managed to delay their executions by "pleading their bellies" – claiming they were pregnant. Under English law, pregnant women could not be executed until after they had given birth. This legal maneuver bought them time, and they were imprisoned in separate cells to await the outcomes of their pregnancies.

Mary Read died in prison, likely from a fever exacerbated by the harsh conditions. Anne Bonny's fate, however, is less clear. There are no definitive records of her execution, leading to various theories about her ultimate fate. Some historians speculate that her father, who still held considerable influence, may have secured her release. According to one popular theory, Anne was released from prison and returned to Charles Town, where she lived out her life under a new identity. Another theory suggests that she escaped and continued her pirate life under a different name.

Regardless of her ultimate fate, Anne Bonny's legacy as a pirate remains enduring and influential. She stands out not only for her daring exploits but also for her defiance of the gender norms of her time. Her partnership with Mary Read and her integral role in Rackham's crew challenge the traditional narratives of piracy as an exclusively male domain. The stories of Anne Bonny and Mary Read highlight the presence of women in piracy and their ability to command respect and fear in a brutal, male-dominated world.

Anne Bonny's life has been immortalized in various works of literature, folklore, and popular culture. Her story has inspired countless retellings, each adding new layers to her legend. In literature, she has been portrayed as a complex and multi-dimensional character, embodying both the romance and the harsh realities of pirate life. In modern popular culture, Anne Bonny has appeared in films, television series, and video games, further cementing her status as an iconic figure in pirate mythology.

The fascination with Anne Bonny also speaks to broader themes of rebellion and empowerment. Her story resonates with those who admire her courage to break free from societal constraints and forge her own path. As a female pirate who defied the expectations of her time, Anne Bonny symbolizes the enduring human spirit's desire for freedom and self-determination.

Chapter 24: Cheung Po Tsai

Cheung Po Tsai, also known as Cheung Po or Zhang Baozai, was one of the most formidable and influential pirate leaders in the South China Sea during the late 18th and early 19th centuries. Born in 1783, Cheung Po Tsai's rise to power and subsequent legacy are emblematic of the complex social, economic, and political dynamics that shaped the maritime history of East Asia. His life, marked by daring exploits, strategic brilliance, and eventual reconciliation with the Qing Dynasty, offers a fascinating narrative of piracy, governance, and adaptation.

Cheung Po Tsai was born into a fishing family in Xinhui, Guangdong Province. His early life was marked by poverty and hardship, common conditions for many coastal families in southern China at the time. The South China Sea, with its intricate network of islands and bustling trade routes, was both a source of livelihood and a region rife with piracy. The socio-economic instability in the region, exacerbated by the decline of the Ming Dynasty and the establishment of the Qing Dynasty, created fertile ground for maritime outlaws.

Cheung Po Tsai's foray into piracy began at a young age when he was captured by the notorious pirate Cheng Yat, also known as Zheng Yi, a formidable pirate leader who commanded a vast fleet known as the Red Flag Fleet. Cheung was forcibly recruited into the pirate's ranks, a common practice among pirate crews seeking to bolster their numbers with skilled sailors and fishermen. Under Cheng Yat's tutelage, Cheung quickly rose through the ranks, demonstrating exceptional leadership and nautical skills.

In 1807, Cheng Yat died, and his widow, Ching Shih (also known as Zheng Yi Sao), assumed command of the Red Flag Fleet. Ching Shih was a formidable leader in her own right, and she recognized Cheung Po Tsai's potential. She adopted him as her son and, in some accounts, made him her lover and second-in-command. This relationship solidified Cheung's position within the fleet and allowed him to further hone his skills as a pirate leader.

Under the joint leadership of Ching Shih and Cheung Po Tsai, the Red Flag Fleet grew to become one of the most powerful pirate confederacies in history. At its height, the fleet boasted hundreds of ships and tens of thousands of pirates. They controlled large swathes of the South China Sea, from the coastal waters of Guangdong and Fujian to the bustling trade routes around the Pearl River Delta. The fleet's dominance was such that it posed a significant threat to the Qing Dynasty's naval forces and the maritime trade of multiple nations, including the British and Portuguese.

Cheung Po Tsai's strategic acumen was instrumental in the fleet's success. He implemented a highly organized structure within the pirate confederacy, establishing a code of conduct that governed the behavior of the pirates and ensured discipline. This code included strict rules regarding the distribution of loot, the treatment of prisoners, and the conduct of the pirates both in battle and in their dealings with local populations. Cheung's leadership ensured that the fleet operated with a level of efficiency and order that was rare among pirate crews.

One of Cheung Po Tsai's most significant achievements was his ability to forge alliances with local communities and officials. Unlike many pirates who relied solely on brute force, Cheung understood the importance of maintaining good relations with the coastal villages and towns that dotted the South China Sea. He often shared a portion of the loot with these communities, earning their support and loyalty. This strategy not only provided the pirates with safe havens and supplies but also made it difficult for the Qing authorities to isolate and defeat them.

Cheung Po Tsai's prowess in naval warfare was demonstrated in numerous battles against the Qing navy and rival pirate fleets. His intimate knowledge of the region's waterways, combined with his tactical brilliance, allowed him to outmaneuver and defeat larger and better-equipped forces. One notable engagement was the Battle of the Tiger's Mouth, where Cheung's fleet decisively defeated a Qing naval force sent to capture him. The battle, fought near the mouth of the Pearl River, showcased Cheung's ability to use the terrain to his advantage, employing hit-and-run tactics and exploiting the Qing navy's unfamiliarity with the local waters.

Despite his successes, Cheung Po Tsai and the Red Flag Fleet faced increasing pressure from the Qing government, which was determined to eliminate the pirate threat. In 1810, the Qing authorities launched a massive campaign to eradicate piracy in the South China Sea. They offered amnesty to pirates who surrendered and severe punishment to those who continued their activities. Recognizing the futility of prolonged resistance against the superior Qing forces, Ching Shih and Cheung Po Tsai decided to negotiate a surrender.

The negotiations were successful, and in 1810, Cheung Po Tsai formally surrendered to the Qing authorities. The terms of the surrender were remarkably lenient. Cheung and his men were allowed to keep their loot and were even given official positions within the Qing administration. Cheung himself was appointed as a naval officer, tasked with combating piracy and maintaining order along the coast. This pragmatic approach by the Qing government helped integrate the pirates into the state's apparatus, turning former adversaries into allies.

Cheung Po Tsai's transition from pirate to naval officer marked a significant turning point in his life. As a commander in the Qing navy, he applied his extensive knowledge of pirate tactics and maritime strategy to his new role. He played a crucial part in the Qing government's efforts to suppress piracy, drawing on his experience and connections to track down and neutralize pirate threats. His expertise was invaluable in securing the maritime trade routes that were vital to the Qing economy.

Cheung Po Tsai's later years were marked by relative stability and respectability. He settled in Guangdong Province, where he continued to serve the Qing government. His transformation from a feared pirate to a respected naval officer is a testament to his adaptability and pragmatism. Cheung Po Tsai's life is a compelling example of how individuals can navigate and survive the shifting currents of political and social change.

Cheung Po Tsai died in 1822, leaving behind a complex legacy. He is remembered both as a ruthless pirate who terrorized the South China Sea and as a skilled leader who brought order and discipline to his fleet. His ability to negotiate a peaceful surrender and transition into a government role underscores the nuanced nature of piracy in the region. Cheung's story reflects the broader themes of survival, adaptation, and the fluid boundaries between legality and outlawry in early 19th-century maritime East Asia.

Cheung Po Tsai's impact on the history and culture of the region is evident in various ways. His name and exploits have been immortalized in folklore, literature, and popular culture. The cave on Cheung Chau Island in Hong Kong, which is said to have been one of his hideouts, remains a popular tourist attraction. The stories of his daring adventures and strategic brilliance continue to captivate and inspire, highlighting the enduring allure of the pirate's life.

Chapter 25: Jean Lafitte

Jean Lafitte, born around 1780 and living until approximately 1823, remains one of the most enigmatic and influential figures in the annals of piracy. His life, a blend of myth and documented history, spans the turbulent years of early 19th-century America and the Caribbean. Lafitte was not merely a pirate but also a privateer, businessman, and patriot who played a crucial role in the War of 1812, showcasing his complex legacy as both a rogue and a hero.

Jean Lafitte's early life is shrouded in mystery, with much of what is known about him derived from a combination of historical records, legends, and Lafitte's own claims. He was likely born in the Basque region of France or Spain, although some accounts suggest he may have been born in the French colony of Saint-Domingue (now Haiti). By the early 1800s, Lafitte, along with his older brother Pierre, had established themselves in the Louisiana Territory, then a region characterized by its strategic importance and rich opportunities for those willing to navigate its complex social and political landscape.

The Lafitte brothers initially operated as privateers, sanctioned by the government of Cartagena (a city-state in modern Colombia) to attack Spanish ships. Privateering was a legally sanctioned form of piracy, where private ship owners were authorized to capture enemy vessels during wartime, selling the captured goods and ships for profit. The distinction between pirate and privateer was often a matter of perspective and legality, subject to the prevailing political winds.

The Lafittes established their base of operations on the island of Barataria, located in the swampy bayous south of New Orleans. Barataria provided an ideal location for their activities, offering natural protection and a strategic position close to major shipping routes and the bustling port of New Orleans. From this base, the Lafittes orchestrated a sophisticated smuggling operation, dealing in contraband goods, including slaves, which they sold to local merchants at prices lower than those demanded by legitimate traders.

Jean Lafitte's operation in Barataria was highly organized and efficient. He maintained a fleet of ships and employed a network of agents and informants to stay ahead of local law enforcement and rival smugglers. Despite the illegal nature of his activities, Lafitte garnered a reputation for fair dealing and reliability, earning the respect and loyalty of many local settlers and merchants. His ability to navigate the intricate social dynamics of the region allowed him to cultivate a broad network of support and influence.

Lafitte's reputation as a shrewd and charismatic leader extended beyond his smuggling operations. He positioned himself as a defender of local interests against the overreach of external authorities, particularly the U.S. federal government, which sought to curtail smuggling and enforce trade regulations. This stance endeared him to many local residents who resented government interference in their affairs.

The War of 1812 marked a turning point in Lafitte's life and legacy. As the conflict between the United States and Great Britain intensified, New Orleans became a critical target for British forces seeking to control the Mississippi River and disrupt American trade. In 1814, the British approached Lafitte, offering him a substantial bribe and land to assist in their planned assault on New Orleans. Lafitte, however, chose to support the American cause, recognizing both the potential for future legitimacy and the alignment of his interests with those of the local population.

Lafitte's decision to aid the United States proved pivotal. He informed Louisiana Governor William C.C. Claiborne of the British plans and offered the services of his men, along with valuable supplies and intelligence, in exchange for a pardon for himself and his crew. Initially met with skepticism, Lafitte's offer was eventually accepted, particularly as the threat of a British attack on New Orleans became imminent.

Lafitte and his men played a crucial role in the defense of New Orleans, culminating in the Battle of New Orleans in January 1815. Under the command of General Andrew Jackson, Lafitte's forces provided essential support in the form of artillery and experienced fighters. The battle, a decisive American victory, not only secured the strategic port city but also elevated Lafitte's status as a local hero. His contribution to the American cause earned him the pardon he sought, and for a time, Lafitte was able to operate with a degree of legitimacy.

Despite his newfound legitimacy, Lafitte's transition to lawful enterprise was short-lived. The conclusion of the War of 1812 and the subsequent enforcement of anti-piracy laws by the U.S. government once again placed him at odds with the authorities. By 1817, Lafitte had relocated his operations to Galveston Island, off the coast of Spanish Texas, where he established a new base known as Campeche.

In Galveston, Lafitte resumed his privateering activities, ostensibly under the flag of the revolutionary Republic of Mexico, which was fighting for independence from Spain. This affiliation provided a veneer of legitimacy, but Lafitte's operations were essentially piratical, targeting ships of various nationalities and selling the plundered goods through a network of contacts. His presence in Galveston drew the ire of the U.S. government, which viewed him as a threat to maritime commerce and regional stability.

In 1820, the U.S. Navy, under the command of Commodore David Porter, moved to eliminate Lafitte's base at Galveston. Given advance warning of the impending action, Lafitte chose to evacuate rather than face destruction. He ordered the burning of Campeche to prevent its use by others and sailed away with his fleet, vanishing into the Caribbean. The final years of Lafitte's life are marked by uncertainty and speculation. Some accounts suggest he continued his piratical activities in the Gulf of Mexico and the Caribbean, while others propose he may have retired to a more quiet life under an assumed identity.

Lafitte's death, like much of his life, is shrouded in mystery. It is generally believed that he died around 1823, possibly in the Yucatan Peninsula or on the island of Cuba. The lack of definitive records and the romanticized nature of his legacy have fueled numerous legends and theories about his final days and possible hidden treasures.

Jean Lafitte's legacy is multifaceted, reflecting the complexity of his character and the turbulent era in which he lived. He is remembered both as a cunning and ruthless pirate and as a savvy businessman and patriot. His ability to navigate the shifting allegiances and political landscapes of his time speaks to his strategic brilliance and adaptability.

In the cultural memory of the Gulf Coast, particularly in Louisiana, Lafitte remains a larger-than-life figure. He has been immortalized in folklore, literature, and popular culture. Lafitte's role in the defense of New Orleans has been celebrated in numerous accounts, often casting him as a swashbuckling hero who defied conventional morality to achieve his ends. His exploits have inspired books, movies, and even theme park attractions, cementing his place in the pantheon of legendary pirates.

Lafitte's impact on the economic and social history of the Gulf Coast is also significant. His smuggling operations facilitated the flow of goods and services in a region where official trade routes were often constrained by war and regulations. By providing a conduit for contraband, Lafitte contributed to the economic vitality of the communities he interacted with, albeit through illicit means.

Moreover, Lafitte's story underscores the blurred lines between piracy and privateering, and between outlaw and patriot. His ability to operate within the legal gray areas of maritime law and his strategic alliances with local and national authorities illustrate the fluid nature of identity and allegiance in the early 19th century.

Chapter 26: Cheng I Sao

Cheng I Sao, also known as Ching Shih or Zheng Yi Sao, was one of the most powerful and successful pirates in history. Born as Shi Xianggu in 1775 in Guangdong Province, China, she began her career in a rather unconventional manner. Before becoming a pirate, she was a prostitute working in a floating brothel. Her life took a dramatic turn in 1801 when she married the notorious pirate Cheng I (Zheng Yi), leader of the Red Flag Fleet. This marriage was not merely a romantic union but also a strategic partnership that would eventually lead to one of the most formidable pirate empires in history.

Upon Cheng I's death in 1807, Cheng I Sao took over his leadership role, demonstrating remarkable acumen and shrewdness. Unlike many widows of her time who might have retreated into the background, Cheng I Sao seized control of the fleet and consolidated her power. She adopted and enforced a strict code of laws, which was one of the key factors in her successful leadership. Her code covered everything from the distribution of loot to the treatment of captives. One of the most notable rules was that captured women were to be treated with respect; anyone who raped a captive woman would be executed. This code fostered loyalty and discipline among her pirates, making the fleet a well-organized and efficient operation.

Under Cheng I Sao's command, the Red Flag Fleet grew to include up to 1,800 ships and an estimated 70,000 men. Her fleet dominated the South China Sea, engaging in piracy, smuggling, and legitimate trade. They attacked the ships of European empires, local merchants, and even the Chinese navy. The fleet's influence extended over the coastal communities, where they demanded tribute and provided protection, effectively operating as a parallel government in some regions. Her fleet was so powerful that it effectively controlled the Guangdong province's coastal waters.

Her ability to maintain control over such a vast and diverse group was due in part to her strategic alliances and political acumen. She collaborated with local officials and corrupt bureaucrats who would turn a blind eye to her activities in exchange for a share of the spoils. This shrewd diplomacy ensured that her operations could continue with minimal interference from the authorities.

In 1810, after years of successful piracy, Cheng I Sao's situation changed when the Chinese government launched a concerted effort to eliminate piracy. Faced with increasing pressure from the Chinese navy, as well as the British and Portuguese, she decided to negotiate a surrender. In a masterstroke of diplomacy, she secured amnesty not only for herself but for her entire crew. The terms of the surrender allowed her and her men to keep their plunder and granted many of them positions within the Qing Imperial Navy. Cheng I Sao's negotiation skills were so effective that she transitioned from being a feared pirate to a respectable member of Chinese society.

After her retirement from piracy, Cheng I Sao continued to lead a prosperous life. She settled in Guangdong, where she ran a gambling house and was involved in the salt trade. Her transition from a feared pirate leader to a successful businesswoman is a testament to her adaptability and intelligence. She lived a long life, dying peacefully in 1844 at the age of 69.

Cheng I Sao's legacy is one of incredible transformation and strategic brilliance. Her rise from a brothel worker to the leader of one of the most formidable pirate fleets in history showcases her remarkable determination and leadership abilities. She managed to outmaneuver and outfight naval forces from multiple nations, maintained a disciplined and loyal fleet, and eventually secured a peaceful and prosperous retirement. Her story is not just one of piracy but of resilience, strategy, and the ability to navigate and manipulate the complex political and social landscapes of her time. Today, Cheng I Sao is remembered as a legendary figure in the annals of piracy, a woman who defied the odds and carved out her place in history with intelligence, courage, and unyielding resolve.

Chapter 27: Rahmah ibn Jabir al-Jalahimah

Rahmah ibn Jabir al-Jalahimah, born around the 1760s, was a formidable pirate and warlord who dominated the Persian Gulf during the late 18th and early 19th centuries. His life and exploits are the stuff of legend, casting a long shadow over the history of piracy in the region. Rahmah's story is one of ambition, conflict, and survival, set against the backdrop of the political and economic upheavals of his time.

Rahmah was born into the Al Jalahimah clan, part of the Bani Khalid tribe, which held significant influence in the Arabian Peninsula. His early years remain shrouded in mystery, but it is known that he began his maritime career at a young age, rapidly rising through the ranks due to his shrewdness and daring. By the late 18th century, Rahmah had become the leader of his clan, guiding them through turbulent times as they sought to expand their power and influence.

The Persian Gulf during Rahmah's time was a vital maritime crossroads, where the interests of regional powers like Persia, Oman, and the emerging British Empire often clashed. Control of the trade routes and pearling industry was crucial, and piracy became a means for local leaders to assert their dominance. Rahmah capitalized on this environment, establishing himself as a pirate with a reputation for both cunning and ferocity.

Rahmah's rise to prominence was marked by his strategic mind and ruthless tactics. He built a fleet of dhows, the traditional sailing vessels of the Gulf, and began launching raids on merchant ships, particularly those under British and Ottoman flags. His knowledge of the Gulf's waters, combined with his tactical acumen, allowed him to evade capture and strike with precision. Rahmah's operations were not solely limited to piracy; he also engaged in legitimate trade, using his gains to finance his raids and expand his influence.

One of Rahmah's most significant accomplishments was his capture of the port town of Khobar in eastern Arabia, which he used as a base for his operations. This stronghold allowed him to exert control over a significant portion of the Gulf, challenging the established powers and drawing the ire of both the British and the Ottomans. Rahmah's audacity and success made him a folk hero to some and a feared adversary to others.

Throughout his career, Rahmah navigated a complex web of alliances and enmities. He was known for his fierce loyalty to his allies and his relentless pursuit of vengeance against his enemies. One of his notable alliances was with the Saudis, who were also seeking to expand their influence in the region. This relationship was mutually beneficial, as Rahmah provided naval support to the Saudis, and in return, they offered him sanctuary and resources.

Rahmah's enmity with the Al Khalifa family of Bahrain was particularly intense. The Al Khalifas, backed by the British, were his primary rivals in the region. Their struggle for dominance over the Gulf was marked by numerous skirmishes and naval battles. Rahmah's most significant confrontation with the Al Khalifas occurred in 1820, during the British-led punitive expedition against piracy in the Gulf. Despite being outnumbered and outgunned, Rahmah's forces fought fiercely, demonstrating his strategic genius and the loyalty he commanded from his men.

The British viewed Rahmah as a significant threat to their interests in the Gulf. His ability to disrupt trade and challenge their naval supremacy made him a prime target. In 1819, the British launched a concerted campaign to eliminate piracy in the Gulf, leading to a series of confrontations. Rahmah, undeterred by the superior firepower of the British navy, continued his resistance, relying on his intimate knowledge of the region's waters and his guerrilla tactics.

Rahmah's end came during the Battle of Khanjar in 1826. Facing a combined British and Ottoman force, Rahmah's fleet was outmatched.

In a final act of defiance, he reportedly tied himself to the mast of his flagship and lit the ship's gunpowder stores, choosing to die by his own hand rather than surrender. This dramatic end cemented his legacy as a fearless and indomitable pirate.

Rahmah ibn Jabir al-Jalahimah's legacy is multifaceted. He is remembered not only as a pirate but also as a symbol of resistance against colonial and imperial powers. His life story encapsulates the tumultuous history of the Persian Gulf during a period of significant change and conflict. Rahmah's ability to navigate the complex political landscape of the time, combined with his tactical brilliance and personal charisma, made him a legend.

The historical accounts of Rahmah's life highlight his strategic mind, his ruthlessness, and his complex character. He was a man who lived by his own code, fiercely loyal to his allies and implacably vengeful towards his enemies. His story is a testament to the turbulent and often violent history of the Persian Gulf, a region where local powers, colonial interests, and economic imperatives collided.

In contemporary times, Rahmah is often celebrated in the Gulf region as a folk hero, a symbol of Arab resistance and resilience. His life has inspired numerous stories, songs, and even academic studies, reflecting his enduring impact on the cultural memory of the region. Rahmah ibn Jabir al-Jalahimah remains an iconic figure, embodying the spirit of a time when the waters of the Persian Gulf were a battleground for power and survival.

Chapter 28: Hippolyte Bouchard

Hippolyte Bouchard, born André Paul Bouchard on January 15, 1780, in Bormes-les-Mimosas, France, was a French-born Argentine sailor and privateer. He is best known for his contributions to the Argentine war of independence and his role in the first Argentine naval campaigns, which took him around the world and earned him a reputation as a daring and skilled maritime commander.

Bouchard's early life in France remains somewhat obscure, but it is known that he joined the French Navy as a young man, where he received his initial naval training and experience. The French Revolution and the subsequent Napoleonic Wars significantly shaped his early career, as France's naval forces were engaged in extensive and often brutal conflicts with various European powers.

In 1809, after a decade of service, Bouchard left France for the New World, initially making his way to the United States. There, he sought opportunities as a privateer, leveraging his naval experience to command ships that preyed on enemy merchant vessels under the authorization of a letter of marque. This practice was common during the era, allowing private ship owners to capture enemy ships and claim them as prizes.

Bouchard's fortunes took a decisive turn when he moved to Buenos Aires, which had recently declared independence from Spain. The newly established United Provinces of the Rio de la Plata were in desperate need of experienced naval officers to defend their coastlines and disrupt Spanish supply lines. Bouchard offered his services to the revolutionary government and quickly rose through the ranks due to his competence and daring.

In 1815, Bouchard was given command of the frigate *La Argentina*, a 34-gun warship tasked with conducting a global campaign against Spanish shipping. This mission was part of the broader strategy of the Argentine independence movement to weaken Spanish colonial rule by disrupting its maritime commerce. Bouchard's global expedition would take him across the Atlantic and Pacific Oceans, making him a prominent figure in the struggle for Latin American independence.

Setting sail from Buenos Aires, Bouchard first targeted Spanish holdings in the Atlantic. His initial successes included capturing several Spanish merchant ships, which not only weakened Spain's economic position but also provided valuable resources for the fledgling Argentine navy. From there, Bouchard rounded Cape Horn and entered the Pacific, where he continued his campaign against Spanish interests.

One of Bouchard's most notable exploits occurred in 1817 when he attacked the Spanish colonial port of El Callao in Peru. Although the assault did not result in the capture of the heavily fortified port, it demonstrated the reach and audacity of the Argentine naval forces. Bouchard's actions in the Pacific were part of a broader strategy to destabilize Spanish control over its American colonies, and his raids had a significant psychological impact on the Spanish authorities.

Bouchard's most famous exploit, however, came in 1818 when he sailed to California, then a remote Spanish province. He allied with local indigenous groups and used the element of surprise to his advantage. On November 20, 1818, Bouchard's forces attacked and captured the Spanish presidio and mission at Monterey. This raid was significant not only for its boldness but also because it marked one of the few times a European settlement on the west coast of North America was taken by force during the era.

During his time in California, Bouchard raised the Argentine flag over Monterey, symbolically claiming the territory for the United Provinces of the Rio de la Plata. His actions were a clear demonstration of Argentina's commitment to disrupting Spanish colonial power far from its own shores. Bouchard also raided other Spanish settlements along the Californian coast, including Santa Barbara and San Juan Capistrano, further weakening Spanish control in the region.

After leaving California, Bouchard continued his privateering activities in the Pacific. He attacked Spanish shipping and settlements in Mexico, Central America, and the Philippines. His campaign disrupted Spanish supply lines and contributed to the broader weakening of Spanish colonial rule in the Americas.

Bouchard's global campaign was not without its challenges. His crew faced harsh conditions, and he often had to deal with the complexities of maintaining a cohesive fighting force far from home. Nevertheless, his leadership and strategic acumen enabled him to achieve significant successes, earning him a reputation as one of the most effective privateers of his time.

In 1820, Bouchard returned to Buenos Aires, where he was hailed as a hero. His exploits had significantly boosted the morale of the Argentine independence movement and demonstrated the potential of the nascent Argentine navy. For his services, he was awarded land and a pension, and he continued to play a role in the development of the Argentine naval forces.

Despite his successes, Bouchard's later life was marked by controversy and hardship. He continued to engage in maritime ventures, but his fortunes waned. In 1837, while involved in a trading expedition in Peru, he was captured by local authorities. He was subsequently imprisoned and later killed during an attempted escape on January 4, 1837.

Hippolyte Bouchard's legacy is a complex one. He is remembered as a daring and skilled naval commander whose actions had a significant impact on the struggle for independence in Latin America. His global campaign against Spanish colonial power demonstrated the potential of naval warfare to influence the course of history. Bouchard's life also highlights the fluid and often precarious nature of maritime ventures during the age of sail, where fortunes could be won and lost through bold actions and strategic brilliance.

In Argentina, Bouchard is celebrated as a national hero. His raids on Spanish settlements and shipping contributed to the broader efforts to secure independence from Spanish rule, and his legacy is honored in various ways, including the naming of streets and naval vessels after him. His story is a testament to the global nature of the struggle for independence in Latin America and the vital role played by privateers and naval forces in shaping the course of history.

Chapter 29: Pedro Gilbert

Pedro Gilbert, often referred to as Don Pedro Gilbert, was a notorious pirate active in the early 19th century. His career as a pirate is most notable for its brutality and the audacious crimes he committed along the Atlantic trade routes, particularly around the coast of Florida and the Caribbean. His exploits have become emblematic of the lawlessness that pervaded the high seas during the so-called "Golden Age of Piracy," albeit occurring towards the latter end of this era.

Pedro Gilbert's early life is somewhat obscure, with scant historical records detailing his origins. He was believed to have been born around the 1800s, likely in Spain, but some sources suggest he might have been Portuguese. Before turning to piracy, Gilbert served as a privateer, a legal form of piracy sanctioned by governments during wartime to disrupt enemy commerce. Privateers were granted letters of marque, which authorized them to attack and capture enemy vessels, keeping a portion of the plunder. However, the transition from privateering to outright piracy was not uncommon, especially in times of peace when such legal endorsements were no longer available.

By the late 1820s and early 1830s, Pedro Gilbert had fully embraced a life of piracy. He commanded a schooner named *Panda*, a swift and well-armed vessel perfectly suited for the hit-and-run tactics typical of pirate operations. Gilbert and his crew preyed on merchant ships traversing the busy trade routes between the Americas and Europe. The *Panda* became a feared name among sailors, notorious for its swift attacks and the ruthless treatment of captured crews.

The most infamous act associated with Pedro Gilbert occurred in 1832. On September 21, 1832, the *Panda* intercepted the American merchant brig *Mexican* near the coast of Florida. The *Mexican*, bound from Salem, Massachusetts, to Rio de Janeiro, was carrying a cargo of silver specie, a valuable target for pirates. Gilbert and his men boarded the *Mexican*, overwhelmed her crew, and seized the treasure. To cover their tracks and eliminate witnesses, the pirates committed a heinous act of cruelty. They set the *Mexican* ablaze with her crew still aboard, leaving them to perish in the inferno.

Remarkably, some of the *Mexican's* crew managed to escape the burning vessel and survived to recount the attack. Their testimony provided crucial evidence that eventually led to Gilbert's downfall. The incident caused an international outcry, with calls for the apprehension and prosecution of those responsible. The brutality of the attack on the *Mexican* highlighted the ongoing threat of piracy and galvanized efforts to eradicate it.

The United States government, in cooperation with British authorities, launched a concerted effort to capture Gilbert and his crew. The Royal Navy, with its superior resources and reach, played a pivotal role in the pursuit. In 1834, the *Panda* was finally captured off the coast of West Africa by the British warship HMS *Curlew*. Gilbert and several of his crew members were apprehended and transported to Boston to stand trial for piracy.

The trial of Pedro Gilbert and his men was a significant event, drawing considerable public attention. In December 1834, they were tried in the United States District Court for the District of Massachusetts. The survivors of the *Mexican* provided compelling testimony, detailing the attack and the horrific conditions they endured. The evidence against Gilbert was overwhelming, and the court found him and his associates guilty of piracy and murder.

On June 11, 1835, Pedro Gilbert and five of his crew members were executed by hanging in Boston. Their execution marked one of the last significant pirate trials in the United States and symbolized the declining era of piracy in the Atlantic. Gilbert's capture and execution were part of a broader effort by international naval forces to suppress piracy, which had plagued maritime trade for centuries.

Pedro Gilbert's legacy is one of infamy. His career as a pirate, marked by the brutal attack on the *Mexican*, exemplifies the violent and lawless nature of piracy during the early 19th century. The capture and prosecution of Gilbert and his crew underscored the growing resolve of nations to combat piracy and secure the seas for legitimate commerce.

Gilbert's life and exploits are often cited in historical accounts of piracy, illustrating the transition from the sanctioned privateering of the 18th century to the outright piracy that persisted into the early 19th century. His story serves as a stark reminder of the perils faced by sailors and merchants during this tumultuous period in maritime history.

In the broader context of pirate lore, Pedro Gilbert stands out as one of the last significant pirates of the Atlantic. His actions and eventual downfall highlight the challenges faced by maritime powers in maintaining law and order on the high seas. The international cooperation that led to his capture reflects the growing importance of collective security and the rule of law in global maritime affairs.

The tale of Pedro Gilbert is a blend of historical fact and maritime legend, embodying the fearsome reputation that pirates held and the relentless efforts to bring them to justice. His execution marked the end of an era, as the golden age of piracy gave way to a more regulated and policed maritime world, paving the way for safer and more reliable sea travel and trade.

Chapter 30: John Bowen

John Bowen, an English pirate who operated during the early 18th century, is a lesser-known but fascinating figure in the annals of piracy. Born around 1681, likely in Bermuda, Bowen's career as a pirate exemplifies the adventurous and often brutal life of those who sought fortune on the high seas during the so-called Golden Age of Piracy. His story, though not as well-documented as some of his contemporaries, provides insight into the complex world of piracy, marked by alliances, betrayals, and the relentless pursuit of wealth.

John Bowen's early life remains largely undocumented, but like many young men of his era, he was likely drawn to the sea by the promise of adventure and riches. The early 18th century was a time of significant maritime activity, with European powers vying for control over trade routes and colonies. Pirates, often operating on the fringes of this colonial expansion, exploited the opportunities presented by this global conflict.

Bowen's career as a pirate began in earnest after he was shipwrecked on Madagascar in 1700. Madagascar was a notorious pirate haven at the time, providing refuge for many of the most infamous pirates of the era. The island's strategic location off the coast of East Africa made it an ideal base for launching attacks on the lucrative trade routes of the Indian Ocean.

After being shipwrecked, Bowen joined the crew of Captain William Read, another pirate operating out of Madagascar. This alliance marked the beginning of Bowen's rise in the pirate ranks. Read's crew soon encountered the pirate Thomas Howard, and Bowen, along with others from Read's crew, joined Howard. This transition demonstrates the fluid nature of pirate allegiances, where crews often merged or split based on opportunities and threats.

Under Thomas Howard, Bowen participated in several successful raids, targeting merchant ships and coastal settlements along the Indian

Ocean. Howard's leadership provided Bowen with valuable experience in navigation, ship handling, and combat, skills that would serve him well in his later career. However, Bowen's time with Howard was short-lived, as Howard eventually retired from piracy, leaving Bowen and the crew to seek new leadership.

Bowen's first significant command came when he was chosen to captain a captured ship, the *Speedy Return*, a former East Indiaman. With the *Speedy Return*, Bowen embarked on a series of raids that would cement his reputation as a daring and successful pirate. He demonstrated a keen understanding of maritime strategy, often employing clever ruses and daring maneuvers to capture his prey.

One of Bowen's most notable exploits occurred in 1701, when he captured the East Indiaman *Pembroke*. The *Pembroke*, heavily laden with valuable cargo, was a significant prize, and its capture underscored Bowen's audacity and tactical prowess. The success of this raid brought considerable wealth to Bowen and his crew, further enhancing his reputation among the pirate community.

Following the capture of the *Pembroke*, Bowen continued to prey on merchant ships traversing the Indian Ocean. His base of operations remained in Madagascar, where he could easily resupply and refit his ships. The island's remote location provided a safe haven from the naval forces of the European powers, which were increasingly focused on suppressing piracy.

Bowen's fleet grew as he captured more ships, and his success attracted a diverse group of followers, including seasoned pirates, escaped slaves, and disenfranchised sailors. This eclectic crew reflected the cosmopolitan nature of pirate society, where individuals from various backgrounds could find common cause in the pursuit of wealth and freedom.

In 1702, Bowen's career took another significant turn when he encountered the pirate, George Booth. Booth, a well-established pirate, offered Bowen the opportunity to join forces, and Bowen agreed. This partnership proved fruitful, as the combined fleets of Bowen and Booth were able to undertake more ambitious raids.

One of their most significant ventures was the capture of the *Defiant*, a heavily armed Dutch East Indiaman. The *Defiant* was a formidable prize, not only for its cargo but also for its potential as a powerful addition to their fleet. The capture of the *Defiant* demonstrated Bowen's increasing boldness and his ability to execute complex operations.

Tragically, George Booth was killed during an attack on Zanzibar in 1704, leaving Bowen to assume full command of their combined forces. This period marked the peak of Bowen's career, as he led his fleet on a series of successful raids across the Indian Ocean. His targets included merchant ships from various European nations, as well as local trading vessels.

Despite his success, Bowen's career was not without challenges. The increasing presence of European naval forces in the Indian Ocean made it more difficult for pirates to operate with impunity. The British, Dutch, and Portuguese navies were all actively engaged in anti-piracy campaigns, seeking to protect their commercial interests and maintain control over vital trade routes.

In response to these threats, Bowen adapted his tactics, often seeking to avoid direct confrontation with naval vessels. He focused on swift, surprise attacks and relied on the speed and maneuverability of his ships to evade capture. This strategy allowed him to continue his piratical activities for several more years.

In 1705, Bowen suffered a significant setback when his flagship, the *Defiant*, was wrecked during a storm off the coast of Madagascar. The loss of the *Defiant* was a severe blow, as it was not only his most powerful ship but also a symbol of his authority. Despite this, Bowen quickly regrouped and captured a replacement vessel, demonstrating his resilience and resourcefulness.

Bowen's later years were marked by increasing pressure from naval forces and dwindling opportunities for piracy. The growing cooperation between European powers in their efforts to suppress piracy made it increasingly difficult for pirates to find safe havens and targets. Recognizing the changing tides, Bowen began to consider retirement.

In 1706, Bowen decided to retire from piracy and settle in Mauritius, another pirate haven. His decision to retire was likely influenced by the increasing risks associated with piracy and the relative security offered by a more stable life on land. Bowen's retirement was relatively short-lived, as he died of an illness in 1707.

John Bowen's career as a pirate, though not as extensively documented as some of his contemporaries, provides valuable insight into the life of a pirate during the early 18th century. His exploits in the Indian Ocean, his alliances with other notorious pirates, and his ability to adapt to changing circumstances highlight the dynamic and often precarious nature of piracy during this period.

Bowen's legacy is that of a skilled and daring pirate who capitalized on the opportunities presented by the turbulent maritime world of the early 18th century. His ability to navigate the complex web of alliances and rivalries among pirates, coupled with his strategic acumen, allowed him to achieve significant success. Though his career was ultimately cut short, Bowen remains a notable figure in the history of piracy, embodying the adventurous and often perilous life of those who sought fortune on the high seas.

Chapter 31: Samuel Bellamy

Samuel Bellamy, commonly known as "Black Sam" Bellamy, is one of the most legendary and romanticized figures in the history of piracy. Born in 1689 in the small English parish of Hittisleigh in Devon, Bellamy's life was marked by adventure, romance, and a meteoric rise to power that has captured the imagination of historians and enthusiasts alike. Despite his brief career, Bellamy became one of the wealthiest pirates in history and left an indelible mark on the Golden Age of Piracy.

Bellamy's early life remains somewhat enigmatic, but it is believed that he went to sea at a young age, likely as a merchant seaman or a sailor in the Royal Navy. The sea was a common career for young men from coastal regions of England, offering both the promise of adventure and the opportunity to escape the rigid class structures of land-based life. This early maritime experience would have equipped Bellamy with the skills and knowledge he would later use to great effect as a pirate.

Around 1715, Bellamy arrived in Cape Cod, Massachusetts. It was here that his life took a dramatic turn, influenced by both romantic and economic factors. According to legend, Bellamy fell in love with Maria Hallett, a young woman from a well-to-do family. The romance between the young, penniless sailor and the wealthy Maria was fraught with societal disapproval. Determined to make his fortune and return to marry her, Bellamy left Cape Cod, driven by both love and ambition.

Bellamy initially headed south to Florida, where he hoped to find employment with the salvors working to recover treasure from the wreck of the Spanish treasure fleet of 1715. This fleet, laden with silver and gold from the New World, had been struck by a hurricane off the coast of Florida, scattering its valuable cargo along the seabed. Many fortune seekers converged on the area, hoping to claim a share of the riches. However, finding the legitimate salvage operations unprofitable or unwelcoming, Bellamy and his companion, the seasoned pirate Paulsgrave Williams, decided to turn to piracy.

By 1716, Bellamy had joined the crew of the pirate Benjamin Hornigold, operating in the Bahamas. The Bahamas, particularly Nassau, had become a notorious pirate haven, a lawless outpost where pirates could rest, refit their ships, and share their plunder. Hornigold was one of the most influential pirates of the time, and under his command, Bellamy honed his skills in piracy. However, Hornigold's reluctance to attack English ships led to a mutiny among his crew, who elected Bellamy as their captain, marking the beginning of his brief but highly successful career as a pirate leader.

Under Bellamy's command, the pirate ship *Mary Anne* (later renamed the *Whydah Gally*) became one of the most feared vessels on the high seas. Bellamy's leadership style was marked by his charismatic and egalitarian approach. He is often remembered for his democratic principles, treating his crew with a level of fairness and equality that was rare for the time. This earned him the nickname "Robin Hood of the Sea," as he was known for his philosophy of redistributing wealth from the rich to the poor. Bellamy's egalitarianism was not just moralistic but also practical, fostering loyalty and morale among his crew.

Bellamy's most famous conquest came in early 1717 when he captured the *Whydah Gally*, a state-of-the-art slave ship. The *Whydah* was en route from Jamaica to England with a valuable cargo of gold, silver, indigo, and other goods. After a fierce battle, Bellamy's men overwhelmed the *Whydah's* crew and claimed the ship and its treasure. Recognizing the superior qualities of the *Whydah*, Bellamy made it his flagship, anointing it with the title of the most powerful pirate ship in the Atlantic. The capture of the *Whydah* significantly boosted Bellamy's wealth and prestige.

Bellamy's success continued as he and his crew plundered ships along the American coast and in the Caribbean. His fleet grew, and his reputation as a formidable and fair pirate spread. He was known for giving captured sailors the choice to join his crew or be set free, a policy that further bolstered his ranks and added to his mythos as a pirate with a sense of honor.

However, Bellamy's meteoric rise was cut tragically short. On April 26, 1717, the *Whydah Gally* was caught in a violent storm off the coast of Cape Cod. Despite Bellamy's skill as a navigator, the ship was driven onto a sandbar and wrecked. The *Whydah* broke apart, and most of the crew, including Bellamy himself, perished in the tumultuous seas. Out of a crew of about 146 men, only two survived. The wreck of the *Whydah* was a catastrophic loss, both in terms of human life and the vast treasure it carried.

The aftermath of Bellamy's death saw a few survivors who managed to tell the tale of the wreck and their captain. One of the survivors, Thomas Davis, a carpenter, provided valuable accounts that helped historians piece together the final moments of the *Whydah* and Bellamy's fate. The survivors were captured by local authorities and put on trial, which was a common fate for captured pirates of the era. These trials often ended in execution, as piracy was a capital offense.

The wreck of the *Whydah* lay undisturbed for more than two centuries, its location and the vast wealth it contained lost to history. It wasn't until 1984 that underwater explorer Barry Clifford discovered the wreck off the coast of Wellfleet, Massachusetts. The discovery of the *Whydah* was a monumental archaeological find, offering a treasure trove of artifacts and providing unprecedented insight into the life and times of Samuel Bellamy and his crew.

Among the artifacts recovered from the *Whydah* were thousands of coins, pieces of jewelry, and everyday items used by the pirates, as well as the ship's bell, which bore the name *Whydah* and confirmed the identity of the wreck. These discoveries have helped historians gain a deeper understanding of the pirate life in the early 18th century and have cemented Bellamy's place in pirate lore.

Samuel Bellamy's legacy is multifaceted. He is remembered not only for his success as a pirate but also for his charismatic leadership and his ideals of equality and fairness. His story, steeped in both historical fact and romantic legend, has inspired countless books, films, and other media, ensuring that the name "Black Sam" Bellamy remains synonymous with the Golden Age of Piracy.

Bellamy's romantic and tragic narrative, combined with his significant achievements, make him one of the most enduring figures in pirate history. His life exemplifies the allure and danger of the pirate's life, marked by moments of great triumph and ultimate tragedy. Bellamy's ideals and the dramatic end of his career continue to captivate the imagination, serving as a poignant reminder of the brief, tumultuous, and often perilous existence of those who chose the path of piracy in the early 18th century.

Chapter 32: Michel de Grammont

Michel de Grammont, born around 1645, was a French privateer and buccaneer who played a significant role in the piracy and privateering activities in the Caribbean and along the Spanish Main during the late 17th century. His career is marked by daring raids, strategic alliances, and a notable impact on the colonial power dynamics of the region. Despite the romanticized accounts of his exploits, Michel de Grammont remains a complex figure whose life was shaped by the turbulent politics and economics of the age.

De Grammont was born into the French nobility in Paris, with some sources suggesting he hailed from an aristocratic family. His full name is often given as Chevalier Michel de Grammont, indicating his noble status. The details of his early life are somewhat obscure, but it is likely that he received a formal education and military training, which was typical for young men of his social standing. This training would have included instruction in navigation, seamanship, and the arts of war, all of which would later prove invaluable in his career as a privateer.

De Grammont's early forays into maritime ventures began in the French Navy, where he served as an officer. However, his career in the navy was cut short due to a dispute with a superior officer. Accounts suggest that de Grammont killed the officer in a duel, an act that forced him to flee France to avoid retribution. This incident marked the beginning of his transition from a naval officer to a privateer and buccaneer.

Seeking refuge and new opportunities, de Grammont made his way to the Caribbean, a region teeming with piracy and privateering. The Caribbean was a hotbed of colonial rivalry, with European powers such as Spain, France, England, and the Netherlands vying for control over lucrative trade routes and territories. Privateers, operating with letters of marque issued by their governments, were authorized to attack and plunder enemy ships and settlements. This quasi-legal form of piracy was seen as a way to weaken rival nations while enriching the privateers and their sponsors.

De Grammont quickly established himself in Saint-Domingue (modern-day Haiti), a French colony that served as a base for many privateers. He obtained a letter of marque from the French governor, giving him legal sanction to attack Spanish ships and settlements. His first notable success came in 1678 when he led a raid on Maracaibo, a Spanish-held city in what is now Venezuela. De Grammont's forces captured the city, looted it, and took hostages for ransom. This raid demonstrated his tactical acumen and boldness, qualities that would define his career.

Following the success at Maracaibo, de Grammont continued his privateering activities with increasing ambition. In 1680, he joined forces with several other notorious buccaneers, including Nicholas Van Hoorn and Laurens de Graaf, to launch an audacious attack on Cartagena, one of the most fortified and wealthy Spanish cities in the Caribbean. The buccaneers managed to breach the city's defenses and capture a significant amount of treasure, further enhancing de Grammont's reputation.

De Grammont's success attracted the attention of the French authorities, who saw him as a valuable asset in their ongoing conflicts with Spain. He was granted further letters of marque and continued to operate with semi-official support. His raids extended beyond the Caribbean to the Gulf of Mexico and the Spanish Main, targeting key ports and trade routes.

One of de Grammont's most daring exploits occurred in 1683 when he led a raid on Veracruz, a major Spanish port on the Gulf of Mexico. Veracruz was a crucial hub for the Spanish treasure fleets, and its capture represented a significant blow to Spanish colonial power. De Grammont's forces managed to seize the city, looting vast amounts of silver and other valuables. However, the raid was not without its challenges. Spanish forces eventually counterattacked, forcing de

Grammont and his men to retreat. Despite the setbacks, the raid on Veracruz solidified de Grammont's status as one of the most formidable privateers of his time.

The latter part of de Grammont's career saw him involved in increasingly larger and more complex operations. He formed alliances with other prominent privateers and buccaneers, creating formidable fleets capable of challenging even well-defended Spanish strongholds. His ability to coordinate and lead multi-national pirate crews showcased his leadership skills and strategic vision.

In 1685, de Grammont participated in one of the largest buccaneer expeditions of the era, an attack on Campeche in the Yucatan Peninsula. This expedition, which included over a thousand men and multiple ships, was a testament to the scale and ambition of de Grammont's operations. The buccaneers captured Campeche, plundering its wealth and further destabilizing Spanish control in the region.

Despite his successes, de Grammont's career was fraught with danger and uncertainty. The shifting political landscape and the growing efforts by European powers to suppress piracy made his activities increasingly perilous. By the late 1680s, the golden age of buccaneering was drawing to a close, as colonial governments sought to establish more control over their territories and trade routes.

In 1686, de Grammont undertook his final known expedition, a raid on the city of St. Augustine in Florida. This raid was part of a broader campaign against Spanish interests in the region. However, details of this expedition are sparse, and it is believed that de Grammont may have perished around this time. Some accounts suggest that he was lost at sea, while others propose that he might have retired or met his end in another manner.

Michel de Grammont's legacy is complex and multifaceted. As a privateer, he operated in a legal gray area, sanctioned by the French government to attack enemy ships and settlements, yet his actions often crossed the line into outright piracy. His daring raids and strategic brilliance earned him both wealth and notoriety, making him one of the most prominent figures in the Caribbean during the late 17th century.

De Grammont's life and exploits also highlight the broader context of piracy and privateering in the Caribbean. His career was shaped by the intense colonial rivalries of the time, where European powers used privateers as instruments of economic warfare. The fluid and often contradictory nature of these activities blurred the lines between legal privateering and piracy, creating a complex and volatile environment.

Despite the romanticized image of pirates and privateers, the reality of their lives was often harsh and brutal. De Grammont's raids involved significant violence, including the looting of cities, taking of hostages, and destruction of property. These actions had profound impacts on the communities he targeted, contributing to the instability and suffering in the region.

Michel de Grammont's story is a testament to the adventurous and dangerous world of the Caribbean in the late 17th century. His career, marked by audacity and strategic prowess, offers a window into the lives of those who navigated the turbulent waters of piracy and privateering. While his fate remains uncertain, his legacy endures as a symbol of the complex interplay between law, commerce, and violence that defined the age of sail.

Chapter 33: Christopher Condent

Christopher Condent, also known as William Condon, was an English pirate who made his mark in the early 18th century, a period often referred to as the Golden Age of Piracy. Condent's career spanned several regions, including the Caribbean, the eastern seaboard of America, and the Indian Ocean, making him one of the few pirates who managed to transition successfully across these different theaters of maritime piracy. His life story provides a fascinating glimpse into the dynamics of piracy, the maritime economy of the time, and the eventual decline of the Golden Age of Piracy.

Christopher Condent was born around the late 1690s, likely in Devon, England, a region known for producing many seafarers and pirates. Little is known about his early life, but it is presumed that he took to the sea at a young age, possibly serving on merchant ships or privateers. This early maritime experience would have provided him with the necessary skills in navigation, ship handling, and combat, all of which would later be essential in his career as a pirate.

Condent's foray into piracy began around 1718, during a time when piracy was rampant in the Caribbean and along the American coast. Following the end of the War of Spanish Succession in 1714, many privateers found themselves out of work and turned to piracy. The Caribbean, with its numerous islands, busy trade routes, and relatively weak colonial defenses, was a prime hunting ground for these pirates.

Condent first appears in historical records as part of a crew that mutinied against their captain while in the West Indies. The details of this mutiny are somewhat murky, but it marked the beginning of Condent's rise in the pirate ranks. After the mutiny, Condent and his fellow pirates captured a ship, which they named the *Fiery Dragon*, and set off on a campaign of plunder and piracy.

The *Fiery Dragon* became Condent's flagship, and under his command, the pirate crew began attacking merchant vessels throughout the Caribbean. Condent quickly gained a reputation for his boldness and tactical acumen. One of his early successes involved capturing a Portuguese ship off the coast of Brazil, which yielded a substantial amount of treasure. This capture not only increased Condent's wealth but also his standing among his fellow pirates.

Following his success in the Caribbean, Condent decided to extend his operations to the West African coast. This decision was likely driven by the increasing naval presence in the Caribbean, as colonial powers began to crack down on piracy. West Africa, with its slave trade and rich coastal cities, offered lucrative opportunities with relatively less risk of encountering heavily armed naval vessels.

In West Africa, Condent and his crew continued their successful campaign, capturing several ships and raiding coastal settlements. Among their notable prizes was a Dutch East Indiaman, which was carrying a valuable cargo of goods from the East Indies. The capture of this ship provided Condent with a considerable fortune and further enhanced his reputation as a formidable pirate.

In 1719, Condent made a strategic move that would define the next phase of his career. He set sail for the Indian Ocean, a region known for its wealth and the relative freedom it offered pirates. The Indian Ocean was a hub of maritime trade, with ships from Europe, the Middle East, and Asia carrying valuable goods such as spices, textiles, and precious metals. The region's vast expanse and numerous islands provided ample opportunities for pirates to hide and resupply.

Condent's decision to move to the Indian Ocean was part of a broader trend among pirates of the time. The Caribbean was becoming increasingly dangerous for pirates due to the concerted efforts of colonial powers to eliminate piracy. The Indian Ocean, by contrast, offered new opportunities and challenges, as well as the possibility of striking at some of the richest trade routes in the world.

Upon arriving in the Indian Ocean, Condent established a base on the island of Madagascar, which had become a notorious pirate haven. Madagascar's strategic location and relative isolation made it an ideal base for pirates to launch attacks on passing merchant ships. From Madagascar, Condent and his crew targeted ships of various nationalities, including English, Dutch, and Indian vessels.

One of Condent's most significant exploits in the Indian Ocean was the capture of an Arab ship off the coast of India. The ship was reportedly carrying a vast treasure, including gold, silver, and precious stones. This haul significantly boosted Condent's wealth and further solidified his reputation as one of the most successful pirates of his time.

Condent's success in the Indian Ocean eventually drew the attention of the European powers, who were keen to protect their lucrative trade routes. In response to the growing threat of piracy, the British, Dutch, and French navies began to increase their presence in the region. These efforts to suppress piracy made the Indian Ocean increasingly dangerous for Condent and his crew.

Recognizing the changing tides, Condent decided to seek a pardon. The practice of offering pardons to pirates was a common strategy used by colonial powers to reduce piracy. By offering a pardon, authorities hoped to entice pirates to give up their illegal activities in exchange for a chance to reintegrate into society without facing prosecution.

In 1720, Condent sailed to Réunion, a French island in the Indian Ocean, to negotiate a pardon. He approached the French governor with an offer to surrender in exchange for amnesty. The governor, recognizing the potential benefits of neutralizing a formidable pirate and recovering some of the plundered wealth, agreed to Condent's terms. Condent was granted a pardon, marking the end of his career as a pirate.

Following his pardon, Condent settled on the island of Réunion, where he lived out the rest of his life in relative obscurity. He used his substantial wealth to establish himself as a respectable member of the colonial society. There are no records of him engaging in further piratical activities, suggesting that he successfully transitioned to a peaceful retirement.

Christopher Condent's story is a testament to the complexities and contradictions of the pirate life during the Golden Age of Piracy. His ability to navigate the treacherous waters of piracy, shifting his operations across different regions, and ultimately securing a pardon, highlights his strategic acumen and adaptability. His career provides valuable insights into the economic and political dynamics of the time, as well as the broader impact of piracy on global trade and colonialism.

Condent's legacy, like that of many pirates, is shrouded in both historical fact and legend. He is often remembered as a daring and successful pirate who managed to amass considerable wealth and outwit the naval forces of his day. His life and exploits continue to capture the imagination, serving as a reminder of the tumultuous and often romanticized world of piracy in the early 18th century.

Chapter 34: Edward Low

Edward Low, commonly known as Ned Low, was one of the most notorious and brutal pirates of the early 18th century. Born around 1690 in Westminster, London, Low's life was marked by violence and ruthlessness, making him one of the most feared figures during the Golden Age of Piracy. His career as a pirate was characterized by a series of audacious raids, relentless cruelty, and a rapid rise and fall that has captured the imagination of historians and pirate enthusiasts alike.

Low was born into a poor family in London, and little is known about his early life. It is believed that he had a rough childhood, which may have contributed to his later violent behavior. By his late teens, Low had moved to Boston in the American colonies, seeking better opportunities. In Boston, he worked as a ship rigger and later as a sailor, gaining valuable experience that would serve him well in his future career as a pirate.

Low's transition from sailor to pirate began around 1721. Dissatisfied with his life and likely influenced by the stories of wealth and adventure associated with piracy, Low joined a group of pirates operating in the Caribbean. His rise in the pirate ranks was swift, and by 1722, he had taken command of his own ship, the *Rebecca*. This marked the beginning of his reign of terror on the high seas.

Low's piracy career was characterized by extreme violence and cruelty, which set him apart from many of his contemporaries. He quickly gained a reputation for his willingness to torture and kill captives, often without provocation. This brutality was not just a means of instilling fear but also a reflection of Low's own volatile and sadistic nature. Stories of his cruelty spread rapidly, making him one of the most feared pirates of his time.

Operating primarily in the Caribbean and along the eastern coast of North America, Low and his crew captured numerous ships, often employing ruthless tactics. One of his early successes was the capture of a Portuguese ship off the coast of Bermuda. The crew of the captured vessel was reportedly treated with exceptional brutality, with many of them being tortured and killed. This incident solidified Low's reputation as a pirate who showed no mercy.

In addition to his cruelty, Low was also known for his strategic acumen and daring. He often used clever ruses to deceive his targets, such as flying false flags or pretending to be a merchant ship. These tactics allowed him to get close to his prey before launching a surprise attack. His ability to outwit and overpower his enemies contributed to his string of successful raids.

Low's flagship, the *Rebecca*, was a swift and well-armed vessel that allowed him to pursue and capture a wide range of targets. Under his command, the *Rebecca* became a symbol of terror for merchant ships and coastal settlements. Low's fleet grew as he captured more ships and recruited new crew members, many of whom were drawn to his reputation for success and his willingness to share the spoils of piracy.

One of the most infamous episodes in Low's career occurred in 1723 when he and his crew attacked a Spanish ship off the coast of Honduras. The Spanish crew was subjected to horrific torture, including mutilation and murder. This incident was widely reported and added to Low's notoriety. His actions drew the ire of colonial authorities and naval powers, who intensified their efforts to capture or kill him.

Despite the increased efforts to hunt him down, Low continued his piratical activities with remarkable boldness. He moved his operations to the Atlantic, preying on ships traveling between Europe and the American colonies. In 1723, he captured a French ship near the Azores, adding to his fleet and increasing his wealth. His raids extended as far as the West African coast, where he targeted slave ships and other valuable cargo vessels.

Low's career, however, was not without its challenges and setbacks. His brutality and unpredictable nature often led to conflicts within his own crew. Mutinies and desertions were common, as even hardened pirates found his methods too extreme. In one notable incident, Low was forced to abandon his ship, the *Rebecca*, after a mutiny. He managed to escape with a small group of loyal followers and soon acquired another vessel, continuing his piracy without missing a beat.

As Low's infamy grew, so did the efforts to capture him. Colonial governors and naval commanders saw him as a significant threat to maritime trade and security. The British Royal Navy, in particular, intensified its patrols and operations aimed at capturing Low and his crew. Rewards were offered for his capture, dead or alive, and the pressure on him increased.

In 1724, Low's luck began to run out. His fleet was significantly weakened after a series of encounters with naval forces and rival pirates. In one such encounter, Low narrowly escaped capture when his ship was overpowered by a British warship. He managed to flee with a small contingent of men, but the incident marked the beginning of the end for his piratical career.

The final blow came later in 1724 when Low and his remaining crew were cornered by a British naval squadron off the coast of Brazil. In the ensuing battle, Low's ship was heavily damaged, and he was forced to abandon it. He and a handful of his men escaped in a small boat, but their fate remains uncertain. Some accounts suggest that Low was eventually captured and executed, while others speculate that he may have continued his piratical activities under a different name or even settled into obscurity.

The legacy of Edward "Ned" Low is one of terror and infamy. His career as a pirate, though relatively short, left a lasting impact on the maritime history of the 18th century. His extreme cruelty and relentless pursuit of plunder set him apart from many of his contemporaries and made him a figure of dread for sailors and settlers alike. His life and actions have been the subject of numerous books, articles, and popular media, cementing his place in the annals of pirate history.

Low's story also highlights the broader context of piracy during the Golden Age. The period was marked by a complex interplay of economic hardship, maritime warfare, and colonial expansion. Pirates like Low thrived in the chaotic environment, exploiting the weaknesses of colonial powers and the vastness of the oceans to carry out their depredations. The response to piracy, in turn, shaped the development of naval strategy and law enforcement in the colonies.

In examining the life of Ned Low, it is important to consider the socio-economic factors that drove many to piracy. The early 18th century was a time of significant upheaval, with wars, trade disputes, and economic instability affecting the lives of many sailors and workers. For individuals like Low, piracy offered a way out of poverty and a means to achieve wealth and notoriety, albeit through violent and illegal means.

Despite his brutal methods, Low's story is a reminder of the human capacity for resilience and adaptation in the face of adversity. His rise from a poor background to become one of the most feared pirates of his time underscores the dynamic and often precarious nature of life during the Golden Age of Piracy. Whether remembered as a villain or a symbol of defiance against the established order, Edward "Ned" Low remains a compelling figure in the history of piracy.

Chapter 35: Samuel Mason

Samuel Mason, born in 1739 in Norfolk, Virginia, was an American frontiersman, soldier, and notorious outlaw who became one of the most feared river pirates in the Ohio River Valley during the late 18th and early 19th centuries. His life spanned the turbulent years of the American Revolution and the early years of the new republic, a period marked by westward expansion, frontier violence, and lawlessness. Mason's transition from soldier and pioneer to criminal mastermind reflects the broader social and economic challenges of this transformative era in American history.

Mason's early life is relatively obscure, but it is known that he was born into a respectable family of Virginia planters. The Mason family, like many others of their class, was involved in agriculture and had connections with the colonial militia. Samuel likely grew up learning the skills necessary for frontier life, including hunting, trapping, and wilderness survival. These skills would later serve him well in his criminal endeavors.

During the American Revolutionary War, Mason joined the Continental Army, where he served with distinction. His military service included participation in several significant battles, and he eventually rose to the rank of captain. This experience not only provided him with combat skills but also introduced him to the chaotic and often brutal realities of frontier warfare. It was during this time that Mason's character began to show signs of the ruthlessness that would later define his career as an outlaw.

After the war, Mason settled in what is now Wheeling, West Virginia, then part of the Virginia frontier. The post-war period was marked by significant social and economic upheaval. Many veterans, including Mason, found it difficult to reintegrate into civilian life. The lack of economic opportunities and the promise of wealth in the untamed western territories led many to move westward in search of a better life.

Mason initially attempted to make an honest living as a farmer and trader, but the harsh realities of frontier life soon drove him to more nefarious pursuits. By the 1790s, he had established himself as a leader of a gang of river pirates operating along the Ohio and Mississippi Rivers. These rivers were major transportation routes for goods and settlers moving west, and they offered lucrative opportunities for those willing to engage in criminal activities.

Mason's gang became infamous for their ruthless tactics and effective organization. They targeted flatboats and keelboats carrying settlers and goods down the rivers, employing deception, violence, and intimidation to seize their prey. The gang would often disguise themselves as friendly traders or settlers, luring their victims into a false sense of security before launching their attacks. This method allowed them to capture numerous boats and accumulate significant wealth.

The gang's base of operations was Cave-in-Rock, a natural cave along the Ohio River in what is now southern Illinois. Cave-in-Rock provided an ideal hideout due to its remote location and natural fortifications. The cave could house a large number of men and supplies, making it a perfect staging ground for raids. From this stronghold, Mason and his men controlled a vast stretch of the river, terrorizing anyone who dared to travel through their territory.

Mason's notoriety grew as reports of his gang's activities spread. They were responsible for countless robberies, murders, and acts of piracy. The gang's brutal methods included torturing their captives to extract information about hidden valuables or simply to instill fear. One of the most infamous practices attributed to Mason's gang was tying their victims to a tree and slashing them with knives, a gruesome fate that ensured their reputation as one of the most feared criminal organizations on the frontier.

Despite their fearsome reputation, Mason and his gang were able to operate with relative impunity for several years. The vast and sparsely populated frontier made it difficult for authorities to mount effective campaigns against them. Additionally, the gang's knowledge of the terrain and their ability to disappear into the wilderness when pursued made them elusive targets. However, the increasing frequency and boldness of their attacks eventually drew the attention of both local militias and federal authorities.

In 1799, a concerted effort was made to eliminate the threat posed by Mason and his gang. A combined force of militia and federal troops launched a series of raids on known hideouts and conducted extensive patrols along the rivers. This campaign resulted in several skirmishes and the capture of some of Mason's men, but the leader himself remained at large. The pressure from law enforcement forced the gang to become even more ruthless in their operations, as they sought to maintain their grip on the region.

By the early 1800s, the relentless pursuit by authorities began to take its toll on Mason's gang. Internal strife and desertions weakened their numbers, and the increasing presence of law enforcement on the rivers made their activities more dangerous. In 1803, Mason decided to move his operations further south, into the Mississippi Territory (modern-day Mississippi and Alabama), hoping to find a more secure base from which to continue his criminal enterprises.

However, this move did not bring the respite Mason had hoped for. The expanding reach of American law enforcement, coupled with the growing determination to eradicate piracy and banditry on the frontier, meant that Mason's days were numbered. In the fall of 1803, he and a small group of loyal followers were captured by a detachment of militia near Natchez, Mississippi. Mason was identified and taken into custody, bringing an end to his reign of terror on the rivers.

Samuel Mason's capture marked a significant victory for law enforcement on the frontier, but it was not the end of his story. While being transported to face trial, Mason managed to escape from custody, demonstrating once again his cunning and resourcefulness. He remained at large for several months, during which time he reportedly continued his criminal activities, albeit on a smaller scale.

Mason's final capture came in 1804 when he was apprehended by Spanish authorities in New Orleans, Louisiana. The Spanish governor, eager to rid the territory of the notorious outlaw, handed him over to American officials. Mason was transported to the federal court in Natchez, where he was tried and convicted of piracy and murder. In 1804, Samuel Mason was executed by hanging, ending the life of one of the most feared and infamous outlaws of the American frontier.

Samuel Mason's legacy is one of violence, lawlessness, and the brutal realities of life on the American frontier. His career as a river pirate highlights the challenges faced by a young nation struggling to establish law and order in its expanding territories. Mason's life also reflects the broader social and economic conditions of the time, as veterans of the Revolutionary War and other displaced individuals sought new opportunities in the West, sometimes turning to crime when legitimate avenues failed.

Mason's story has been the subject of numerous books, articles, and even folklore, contributing to the mythos of the American frontier outlaw. His life, marked by both military service and ruthless criminality, offers a window into the complexities of frontier society and the thin line between survival and lawlessness. The tale of Samuel Mason serves as a reminder of the turbulent and often violent history of America's westward expansion and the enduring fascination with the figures who lived on the fringes of that era.

Chapter 36: Howell Davis

Howell Davis, born around the 1690s, was a Welsh pirate whose brief but notable career left a significant mark on the Golden Age of Piracy. His story is one of daring exploits, clever deceptions, and eventual betrayal. Despite his relatively short life, Davis's legacy is rich with tales of cunning and adventure, illustrating the complex and often romanticized world of early 18th-century piracy.

Davis was born in Milford Haven, Pembrokeshire, Wales, a region known for its seafaring traditions. Little is known about his early life, but it is likely that he was drawn to the sea at a young age, given his later expertise in navigation and maritime tactics. Before turning to piracy, Davis worked as a mate on merchant ships, a position that would have given him extensive knowledge of the shipping routes and the intricacies of maritime trade.

His transition to piracy occurred somewhat by chance. In July 1718, Davis was serving as the mate of a slaving ship called the *Cadogan*, which was captured by the notorious pirate Edward England off the coast of West Africa. England's crew, recognizing Davis's talents and leadership qualities, offered him a choice: join them or face an uncertain fate. Davis chose the former, thus beginning his career as a pirate.

Davis quickly distinguished himself among the pirate ranks. He was known for his charm, intelligence, and particularly his gift for deception. Unlike many of his contemporaries who relied on brute force, Davis often used cunning and guile to achieve his ends. One of his most famous tactics was to pose as a legitimate privateer or merchant captain, gaining the trust of his targets before revealing his true intentions. This method allowed him to capture several ships with minimal resistance.

After a few months with England, Davis struck out on his own. He captured a sloop off the coast of Guinea and renamed it the *Buck*. With this vessel, he began a series of successful raids along the West African coast, targeting both European and African ships. His charismatic leadership and strategic acumen quickly attracted a loyal crew, many of whom were experienced seamen disillusioned with their previous lives.

One of Davis's most notable early successes was the capture of the *Princess*, a large and well-armed Portuguese ship. Using his signature deception, Davis approached the *Princess* flying British colors and convinced the captain that he was a legitimate privateer. Once on board, Davis and his men overpowered the crew and seized the ship, which they found to be laden with valuable cargo. This capture not only enriched Davis and his crew but also enhanced his reputation as a pirate captain of considerable skill.

Following the capture of the *Princess*, Davis sailed to the Cape Verde Islands, where he continued his piratical activities. His growing notoriety attracted the attention of other pirate leaders, including the infamous Bartholomew Roberts, who would later rise to even greater fame. Davis and Roberts met in 1719, and the two quickly formed an alliance. Roberts joined Davis's crew, and the two pirates embarked on a series of daring raids together.

Davis's partnership with Roberts was particularly fruitful. The two captains shared a similar approach to piracy, favoring strategy and deception over outright violence whenever possible. This approach allowed them to capture several valuable prizes, including the *Royal Africa Company* ship *Gambia Castle*, which they took by posing as British naval officers. The capture of the *Gambia Castle* was a significant coup, as it was heavily armed and well-defended. Davis's ability to take the ship with minimal bloodshed underscored his reputation as a master of deceit.

Despite his successes, Davis's career was not without its challenges. The increasing presence of European naval forces in the region made piracy more dangerous, and the constant threat of capture loomed large. To mitigate these risks, Davis moved his operations to the

Caribbean, where he hoped to find easier targets and fewer naval patrols.

In the Caribbean, Davis continued his successful run, capturing several ships and raiding coastal settlements. One of his most daring exploits occurred in the summer of 1719 when he and his crew attacked the island of Principe, a Portuguese stronghold. Using his usual tactics, Davis posed as a merchant captain seeking to trade. He gained entry to the island's main fort, where he and his men overpowered the garrison and looted the settlement. The raid on Principe demonstrated Davis's boldness and his ability to carry out complex operations with precision.

However, Davis's luck began to run out later that year. In October 1719, he attempted to capture the Portuguese fort at Gambia. The operation started well, with Davis using his familiar ruse of posing as a legitimate captain. He managed to infiltrate the fort and take control of it briefly, but the situation quickly deteriorated. The Portuguese garrison mounted a fierce counterattack, and Davis was unable to maintain his hold on the fort.

In the ensuing battle, Davis was mortally wounded by a musket shot. His men, caught off guard by the intensity of the Portuguese resistance, were forced to retreat, leaving their captain behind. Davis's death marked the end of his piratical career, but his legacy lived on, particularly through his association with Bartholomew Roberts.

Roberts, inspired by Davis's example and tactics, went on to become one of the most successful and feared pirates of the Golden Age. He adopted many of Davis's strategies, including the use of deception and strategic planning, and led a series of highly successful raids across the Atlantic. Roberts's eventual capture and execution in 1722 marked the end of an era, but his exploits, along with those of Howell Davis, continued to capture the popular imagination.

Davis's story is a testament to the complex and multifaceted nature of piracy during the early 18th century. Unlike the stereotypical image of the bloodthirsty pirate, Davis combined charm, intelligence, and ruthlessness in equal measure. His ability to manipulate and deceive his enemies set him apart from many of his contemporaries and contributed to his considerable success.

Moreover, Davis's life underscores the broader social and economic context of the time. The early 18th century was a period of significant upheaval, marked by wars, economic hardship, and the expansion of European colonial empires. Many individuals, like Davis, turned to piracy as a means of survival and resistance against the rigid social and economic structures of the time.

Chapter 37: Israel Hands

Israel Hands, also known as Basilica Hands, is a name that resonates through the annals of pirate history primarily due to his association with one of the most infamous pirates of all time, Edward Teach, better known as Blackbeard. While less is known about Hands compared to other pirates of the era, his career provides a fascinating glimpse into the world of piracy during the early 18th century. His story, interwoven with that of Blackbeard, captures the tumultuous and often violent life of pirates during the Golden Age of Piracy.

Israel Hands was born around the late 17th century, though the exact date and location of his birth remain uncertain. Like many pirates, Hands' early life is shrouded in mystery. It is likely that he began his maritime career in the merchant or naval service, gaining the seafaring skills that would later serve him in his piratical endeavors. His transition to piracy, as was common at the time, was probably driven by the economic hardships and limited opportunities available to sailors.

Hands' first significant appearance in historical records comes with his association with Blackbeard. Blackbeard, whose real name was Edward Teach (or Thatch), was one of the most feared and renowned pirates of the Golden Age. By 1717, Blackbeard had established himself as a formidable pirate captain, and it was during this period that Hands joined his crew. Hands quickly rose through the ranks, earning Blackbeard's trust and becoming one of his most loyal lieutenants.

Hands' role in Blackbeard's crew was significant. He served as the second-in-command and was often entrusted with important tasks and command of captured ships. One of his most notable assignments was as the captain of Blackbeard's flagship, the Queen Anne's Revenge, when Blackbeard was not aboard. This position underscored the trust and confidence Blackbeard placed in Hands, as the Queen Anne's Revenge was a heavily armed former French slave ship that Blackbeard had captured and modified for his purposes.

In late 1717 and early 1718, Blackbeard and his fleet, including Hands, wreaked havoc along the eastern coast of the American colonies and in the Caribbean. They captured numerous vessels, plundering their cargoes and often employing brutal tactics to instill fear in their victims. Blackbeard's fearsome reputation was bolstered by his terrifying appearance and his strategic use of psychological warfare. Hands, as his trusted lieutenant, played a key role in these operations.

One of the most infamous episodes involving Hands occurred during the blockade of Charleston, South Carolina, in May 1718. Blackbeard's fleet, which included the Queen Anne's Revenge, blockaded the port for several days, capturing ships attempting to enter or leave the harbor. The pirates' primary objective was to secure medical supplies, but they also took hostages, including prominent citizens of Charleston. Hands was likely involved in the negotiation and coordination of this audacious blockade, which ended successfully for the pirates, who received the demanded supplies and released the hostages.

Following the blockade of Charleston, Blackbeard and his fleet sailed north to North Carolina. In June 1718, disaster struck when the Queen Anne's Revenge ran aground and was wrecked off the coast of Beaufort Inlet. The exact circumstances of the wreck remain unclear, but it is speculated that Blackbeard may have deliberately grounded the ship to downsize his crew and increase his share of the loot. Hands, commanding the sloop Adventure at the time, survived the wreck and continued to serve under Blackbeard.

After the loss of the Queen Anne's Revenge, Blackbeard and Hands continued their piratical activities. However, the increased pressure from colonial authorities made their operations more perilous. In November 1718, Blackbeard met his end in a fierce battle with British naval forces led by Lieutenant Robert Maynard off Ocracoke Island, North Carolina. During the battle, Blackbeard was killed, and his crew, including Hands, was captured or killed.

Israel Hands' fate following Blackbeard's death is somewhat murky. According to some accounts, Hands was captured and taken to Virginia, where he was held for trial. He had suffered a severe leg injury, reportedly inflicted by Blackbeard himself in a fit of drunken rage. This injury may have spared Hands from execution, as he was seen as less of a threat. In an unusual twist of fate, Hands testified against corrupt officials during the trials, which may have contributed to his eventual release.

After his release, Hands disappeared from the historical record. His later life remains a mystery, and it is unclear whether he returned to piracy, sought a more legitimate occupation, or met an unknown fate. The lack of records suggests that Hands either managed to evade further notice or died shortly after his release. His life after piracy remains one of the many unanswered questions about the Golden Age of Piracy.

Israel Hands' legacy is intertwined with that of Blackbeard, and his story provides valuable insights into the life of pirates during the early 18th century. The period was marked by widespread economic disparity, colonial expansion, and the struggle for control over trade routes. Pirates like Hands and Blackbeard exploited these conditions, seeking wealth and freedom on the high seas. Their actions challenged the established order and highlighted the lawlessness and unpredictability of the maritime world.

The life of Israel Hands also illustrates the hierarchical structure and complex social dynamics within pirate crews. Hands' rise to a position of authority under Blackbeard demonstrates the meritocratic nature of pirate society, where skill, loyalty, and bravery were rewarded. At the same time, the often brutal and precarious nature of pirate life is evident in Hands' experiences, from his rise to prominence to his ultimate fall and uncertain fate.

Hands' story has been romanticized and fictionalized over the centuries, contributing to the enduring fascination with pirate lore. His character has appeared in various books, films, and other media, often depicted as a quintessential pirate figure loyal to his notorious captain. This portrayal, while sometimes exaggerated, reflects the lasting impact of Hands and his contemporaries on popular culture and the collective imagination.

Chapter 38: Anne Dieu-le-Veut

Anne Dieu-le-Veut, born around 1661 in France, stands out as one of the few well-documented female pirates of the 17th century. Her life and career provide a fascinating glimpse into the often-overlooked role of women in the Golden Age of Piracy, a period typically dominated by tales of male buccaneers. Dieu-le-Veut's story is one of resilience, daring, and fierce independence, set against the backdrop of the Caribbean's turbulent waters and the broader geopolitical struggles of the era.

Anne Dieu-le-Veut's early life remains largely shrouded in mystery, typical of many historical figures from the 17th century, especially women. Her birth name, family background, and early years are not well-documented. However, it is known that she was born in France and that her life took a dramatic turn when she was transported to the Caribbean. As with many women of her time, Dieu-le-Veut likely faced limited opportunities and harsh living conditions, which may have driven her towards a life of piracy.

Anne's life changed irrevocably when she was sent to the French colony of Tortuga, an island off the coast of Haiti, which was a notorious haven for pirates and privateers. Tortuga attracted a motley assortment of outlaws, adventurers, and fortune seekers. The island was a strategic base for launching raids against Spanish shipping and settlements, making it a key player in the broader conflicts between European powers vying for control in the New World.

It was in Tortuga that Anne Dieu-le-Veut met her first husband, Pierre Length. Details about Length are sparse, but he was likely involved in the island's piratical activities. Their marriage, however, was short-lived; Length was killed in a duel, a common occurrence in the rough-and-tumble world of Tortuga. Anne's response to her husband's death was anything but typical for a woman of her time. Instead of retreating into widowhood, she challenged the man who had killed her husband, Laurens de Graaf, to a duel herself.

Laurens de Graaf, a formidable pirate in his own right, was so impressed by Anne's courage and determination that he refused to fight her and instead proposed marriage. Anne accepted, and their union became one of the most famous pirate partnerships in history. Together, Anne and Laurens de Graaf embarked on numerous piratical exploits, becoming a powerful force in the Caribbean.

Anne Dieu-le-Veut's participation in piracy was exceptional for several reasons. During the 17th century, piracy was an overwhelmingly male-dominated enterprise. Women were often seen as bad luck on ships and were generally excluded from maritime ventures. However, Anne defied these conventions. She not only accompanied her husband on his expeditions but also took an active role in the planning and execution of their raids. Her involvement ranged from managing logistics to participating in battles, demonstrating her versatility and resourcefulness.

One of the most notable aspects of Anne's career was her involvement in the raid on Veracruz in 1683. Veracruz was a major Spanish port city on the Gulf of Mexico, and its capture required careful planning and bold execution. Laurens de Graaf led a coalition of pirates, including Anne, in a daring assault on the city. They managed to breach the city's defenses and occupy Veracruz for several days, during which they looted the town and took numerous hostages for ransom. This raid was one of the most audacious and successful pirate attacks of the era, showcasing Anne's willingness to engage directly in combat and her strategic acumen.

Following the raid on Veracruz, Anne and Laurens continued their piratical activities, targeting Spanish and other European ships and settlements throughout the Caribbean. Their exploits brought them wealth and notoriety, but also made them targets for the increasingly coordinated efforts by colonial authorities to suppress piracy. The early

1690s saw a concerted effort by European powers to clamp down on piracy, and the Caribbean became a more dangerous place for even the most successful pirates.

In the midst of these challenges, Anne Dieu-le-Veut's resilience and leadership became even more apparent. She and Laurens de Graaf continued to elude capture and maintain their piratical activities despite the increased risks. Anne's role was not just that of a supportive partner; she was a leader in her own right, commanding respect and loyalty from their crew. Her ability to navigate the perilous waters of piracy, both literally and figuratively, underscores her formidable presence in a world that was heavily biased against women.

Anne Dieu-le-Veut's life took another dramatic turn when Laurens de Graaf was reportedly killed in battle around 1694. Some accounts suggest that he may have died earlier, in 1692, during a raid on the Spanish town of Saint Augustine in Florida. The exact circumstances and date of his death remain uncertain, adding an element of mystery to their story. Following her husband's death, Anne's fate becomes less clear. There are conflicting reports about her later life. Some sources suggest that she continued to engage in piracy independently, while others indicate that she may have retired from the pirate life.

One account suggests that Anne returned to the French colony of Saint-Domingue (modern-day Haiti), where she lived out her remaining years. If this account is accurate, it would mean that Anne managed to survive the perilous world of piracy and find some measure of peace and stability. However, the lack of concrete evidence about her later years leaves much about her ultimate fate to speculation.

Anne Dieu-le-Veut's legacy is significant for several reasons. First, she stands as a rare example of a female pirate who not only participated in but also thrived within the male-dominated world of 17th-century piracy. Her courage, intelligence, and leadership challenged the gender norms of her time and demonstrated that women could play active and influential roles in piracy.

Second, Anne's life and career highlight the broader socio-political context of the Golden Age of Piracy. The Caribbean during this period was a volatile region, with European powers vying for control and pirates exploiting the resulting chaos. Anne and her contemporaries navigated this complex landscape, seizing opportunities and asserting their independence in ways that defied the established order.

Third, Anne's story contributes to the rich tapestry of pirate lore that continues to captivate the popular imagination. Her exploits, alongside those of other famous pirates, have been romanticized and mythologized over the centuries, inspiring countless books, films, and other media. While the historical record provides only glimpses of her life, these glimpses are enough to paint a picture of a formidable and fascinating woman who carved out her own place in a dangerous and unpredictable world.

Chapter 39: Francis Spriggs

Francis Spriggs, a pirate active during the early 18th century, is a figure whose life and career encapsulate many of the key elements of the Golden Age of Piracy. While not as famous as some of his contemporaries, such as Blackbeard or Bartholomew Roberts, Spriggs nonetheless carved out a notorious reputation for himself. His exploits, marked by audacity, brutality, and a keen strategic mind, provide valuable insights into the pirate world of his time. This detailed account aims to explore Spriggs' background, his rise to infamy, his notable exploits, and his ultimate fate, while situating his story within the broader context of early 18th-century piracy.

Francis Spriggs' early life is largely undocumented, which is not uncommon for pirates of the time. Born sometime in the late 17th century, likely in England, Spriggs' early experiences at sea would have been shaped by the harsh realities of maritime life during this period. Many sailors faced poor conditions, low wages, and brutal discipline, which made piracy an attractive alternative for those seeking freedom and wealth. It is probable that Spriggs served on merchant or naval vessels before turning to piracy, gaining the nautical skills that would later serve him well.

Spriggs first appears in historical records in connection with the notorious pirate Edward Low, also known as Ned Low. Low was an infamous pirate captain known for his viciousness and cruelty. Spriggs initially served as Low's quartermaster, a position of significant authority and responsibility within a pirate crew. The quartermaster was often second only to the captain and was responsible for maintaining order, dividing loot, and representing the crew's interests. This role suggests that Spriggs was highly respected and trusted by his fellow pirates.

Spriggs' association with Edward Low was pivotal in his development as a pirate leader. Low's ferocious tactics and strategic acumen left a lasting impression on Spriggs. Together, they conducted numerous raids in the Atlantic and Caribbean, targeting ships of various nationalities. The success of these operations depended on a combination of boldness, cunning, and an intimate knowledge of maritime routes and conditions.

Around 1724, Spriggs decided to strike out on his own. The exact reasons for his departure from Low's crew are not clear, but it may have been due to a desire for greater autonomy or differences in leadership style. Whatever the cause, Spriggs took command of a captured vessel, which he named the *Sea Flower*, and began his independent career as a pirate captain.

Spriggs quickly established a reputation for brutality and efficiency. One of his early exploits as captain was the capture of the British sloop *John and Elizabeth*. After taking the ship, Spriggs and his crew subjected the captured crew to torture and interrogation, a common tactic to extract information about valuable shipping routes and cargoes. The brutal treatment of prisoners was a hallmark of Spriggs' approach to piracy, reflecting the ruthless environment in which he operated.

One of Spriggs' most infamous actions was the capture and destruction of the merchant ship *Mary*. After looting the vessel, Spriggs and his crew set it on fire, a tactic designed to instill fear and discourage resistance among future targets. This kind of wanton destruction was characteristic of Spriggs' reign of terror on the high seas. The psychological impact of his actions was significant, as the threat of torture and execution made many merchant crews more likely to surrender without a fight.

Spriggs' piracy was not confined to the Atlantic. He and his crew ventured into the Caribbean, a region teeming with potential targets due to the dense traffic of merchant and naval ships. The Caribbean was a hotbed of pirate activity during the early 18th century, with numerous islands providing safe havens and opportunities for refitting and resupplying. Spriggs took advantage of these conditions to expand his operations and maximize his plunder.

One of Spriggs' notable Caribbean exploits was the capture of the *Fortune*, a ship belonging to the South Sea Company. This British trading company was involved in the lucrative trade of slaves and goods between Africa, the Americas, and Europe. The *Fortune* was laden with valuable cargo, and its capture was a significant coup for Spriggs and his crew. The success of such raids not only brought immediate wealth but also helped to build Spriggs' reputation among his peers and potential recruits.

Despite his successes, Spriggs' career was fraught with challenges. The increasing presence of naval patrols and privateers made piracy more dangerous. The British, in particular, were intensifying their efforts to suppress piracy, deploying warships and offering pardons to those willing to abandon their criminal ways. Spriggs, like many pirates, faced the constant threat of capture and execution.

Spriggs' response to these challenges was characteristic of his ruthless pragmatism. He continued to employ brutal tactics to maintain discipline and deter mutiny within his crew. Accounts from the time describe Spriggs as a harsh disciplinarian, willing to use extreme measures to enforce his authority. This approach, while effective in the short term, also created an atmosphere of fear and resentment that could undermine long-term loyalty.

The exact details of Spriggs' later career and eventual fate are somewhat obscure, as records from the period are often incomplete or contradictory. Some sources suggest that he continued his piratical activities well into the late 1720s, while others imply that he may have been captured or killed earlier. One account indicates that Spriggs was captured by the Royal Navy and hanged, though the specific circumstances of his capture and execution are not well-documented.

Spriggs' legacy as a pirate is marked by his strategic acumen and brutal tactics. His ability to command and intimidate his crew, coupled with his daring raids on merchant shipping, ensured his place in the annals of pirate history. Spriggs operated during a time when piracy was both a significant threat to maritime trade and a form of resistance against the rigid social and economic hierarchies of the time.

The broader context of Spriggs' career is essential to understanding his actions and motivations. The early 18th century was a period of intense maritime competition and conflict. European powers were vying for dominance in the Americas, Africa, and Asia, leading to frequent wars and the disruption of trade routes. The economic pressures and opportunities created by this environment made piracy an appealing option for many sailors.

Pirates like Spriggs exploited the weaknesses and vulnerabilities of the maritime world. They targeted the wealth flowing from the colonies to Europe, attacking ships laden with goods, slaves, and precious metals. Their activities disrupted trade and forced merchant companies and governments to invest heavily in naval defenses and anti-piracy measures.

Spriggs' career also highlights the complex social dynamics within pirate communities. While often depicted as anarchic and lawless, pirate crews operated according to their own codes of conduct and governance. Positions like the quartermaster and captain were typically elected by the crew, and decisions were often made collectively. This democratic aspect of pirate life contrasted sharply with the hierarchical structures of naval and merchant ships.

Chapter 40: Thomas Anstis

Thomas Anstis, an English pirate who operated during the early 18th century, represents a fascinating figure from the Golden Age of Piracy. His career, marked by loyalty, mutiny, and a series of successful raids, provides a compelling narrative of life on the high seas during one of the most tumultuous periods in maritime history. While not as notorious as some of his contemporaries, such as Blackbeard or Bartholomew Roberts, Anstis' story is rich with the intrigue, danger, and adventure that characterize the era.

Born around the 1690s, Thomas Anstis' early life remains largely undocumented. Like many pirates of his time, details about his upbringing and the circumstances that led him to a life of piracy are scarce. It is likely that Anstis began his maritime career in the Royal Navy or on merchant ships, as was common for many who later turned to piracy. The harsh conditions, low pay, and brutal discipline experienced by sailors often made the lure of piracy—a life promising freedom, adventure, and potential wealth—irresistible.

Anstis first emerges in historical records as a member of the crew under the infamous pirate captain Bartholomew Roberts. Roberts, also known as Black Bart, was one of the most successful and feared pirates of the Golden Age, capturing over 400 ships in his career. Anstis served as the first mate aboard the *Royal Rover*, Roberts' flagship. His close association with Roberts provided him with invaluable experience and exposure to the strategies and operations of high-seas piracy.

The year 1721 marked a significant turning point in Anstis' career. While cruising off the coast of West Africa, a schism developed within Roberts' crew. Discontent with Roberts' leadership and perhaps motivated by a desire for greater autonomy and spoils, Anstis led a mutiny against him. Seizing the sloop *Morning Star*, Anstis and a group of loyal followers broke away from Roberts' command, striking out on their own. This act of defiance set the stage for Anstis' career as an independent pirate captain.

After the mutiny, Anstis and his crew sailed to the Caribbean, a region teeming with potential targets due to its heavy maritime traffic. They renamed their ship the *Good Fortune* and embarked on a series of raids against Spanish and British vessels. The Caribbean offered a strategic advantage with its numerous islands providing hiding places and bases of operations, as well as abundant merchant shipping routes ripe for plunder.

One of Anstis' early successes as captain came with the capture of a Portuguese vessel laden with valuable cargo. This significant haul boosted the morale of his crew and affirmed Anstis' capabilities as a leader. His tactical acumen and ability to inspire his men were crucial in maintaining the loyalty and cohesion of his pirate band, which was essential in the cutthroat world of piracy.

Anstis' exploits continued as he targeted ships across the Caribbean and the Atlantic. His tactics were marked by cunning and ruthlessness, employing strategies such as surprise attacks and overwhelming force to subdue his prey. The wealth accumulated from these raids allowed Anstis to maintain his crew and keep his ship well-armed and provisioned.

Despite his successes, Anstis' career was fraught with challenges. The early 1720s saw increasing efforts by colonial powers to suppress piracy. The British, in particular, intensified their naval patrols and offered pardons to pirates willing to surrender and abandon their criminal ways. These measures made the pirate life increasingly perilous, as naval forces became more adept at hunting down and capturing pirate ships.

In response to these pressures, Anstis and his crew adopted a strategy of evasion and relocation. They often sought refuge in the remote coves and inlets of the Caribbean islands, utilizing their intimate knowledge of the region to avoid detection. This cat-and-mouse game with the authorities required constant vigilance and adaptability, underscoring the precarious nature of piratical existence.

One of the most dramatic episodes in Anstis' career occurred in 1722 when his ship, the *Good Fortune*, was pursued by HMS *Winchelsea*, a British man-of-war. Anstis managed to elude capture by navigating into shallow waters where the larger warship could not follow. This narrow escape highlighted Anstis' navigational skills and quick thinking, but it also underscored the increasing danger posed by naval forces.

Following this close call, Anstis and his crew decided to seek a royal pardon, hoping to secure their safety and possibly reintegrate into legitimate society. They sailed to the uninhabited island of Blanquilla, off the coast of Venezuela, to await news of their petition. During this period of inactivity, discipline among the crew began to deteriorate. The lack of plunder and the uncertainty of their situation led to restlessness and infighting.

While on Blanquilla, Anstis received news that their request for a pardon had been denied. This rejection was a severe blow, leaving the crew with little choice but to resume their piratical activities. They set sail once more, seeking targets to replenish their dwindling supplies and morale. Despite the setback, Anstis remained resolute, continuing to lead his men with determination.

In 1723, Anstis' luck ran out. While anchored off the coast of the Bahamas, his ship was surprised and attacked by a British naval vessel. The ensuing battle was fierce, but Anstis' ship was ultimately overpowered. Many of his crew were killed or captured, and Anstis himself was taken prisoner. He was transported to Nassau, where he faced trial for piracy. The trial was swift, and Anstis was found guilty. He was hanged later that year, bringing an end to his tumultuous career.

The life of Thomas Anstis offers a vivid window into the world of 18th-century piracy. His journey from a subordinate under Bartholomew Roberts to an independent pirate captain illustrates the fluid and often treacherous nature of pirate hierarchies. Anstis' ability to lead a mutiny, command a ship, and conduct successful raids speaks to his leadership and nautical skills.

Anstis' career also highlights the broader socio-economic context of the Golden Age of Piracy. The early 18th century was a time of significant maritime expansion and conflict. European powers, particularly Britain, Spain, and France, were engaged in a relentless struggle for dominance over trade routes and colonies. This environment created opportunities for pirates to exploit the vulnerabilities of merchant shipping and colonial defenses.

Pirates like Anstis operated in a world where the boundaries between legality and criminality were often blurred. Privateering, sanctioned by governments during wartime, was a closely related activity, and many pirates had previous experience as privateers. The transition from privateering to piracy was sometimes a matter of circumstance and opportunity rather than a deliberate choice.

The story of Thomas Anstis also underscores the precariousness of the pirate life. Despite the potential for immense wealth, the risks were high. Pirates faced the constant threat of capture, execution, or death in battle. The internal dynamics of pirate crews were complex, with issues of discipline, loyalty, and leadership playing crucial roles in their survival and success.

Anstis' attempts to secure a pardon and reintegrate into legitimate society reflect the ambivalence many pirates felt about their chosen path. The allure of freedom and fortune was tempered by the harsh realities of living outside the law. The rejection of their pardon petition and the subsequent return to piracy highlight the limited options available to those who had crossed the line into criminality.

Chapter 41: Henry Every

Henry Every, also known as Henry Avery, and by the moniker "Long Ben," is one of the most notorious and enigmatic figures of the Golden Age of Piracy. Born in 1659 in Newton Ferrers, near Plymouth, England, Every's life was a tapestry of daring escapades, immense wealth, and an eventual disappearance that has fueled centuries of speculation and legend. Every's career, which spanned only a few years, left an indelible mark on piracy history and had significant repercussions for the British East India Company and Anglo-Indian relations.

Henry Every's early life remains largely undocumented, which is not uncommon for many historical figures of the time, particularly those who later turned to piracy. It is known that he came from a seafaring background, possibly working on merchant and naval ships. His early experiences at sea would have equipped him with the necessary skills and knowledge that later proved invaluable in his piratical career.

Every first comes into clear historical focus in the early 1690s. By this time, he had gained considerable experience at sea, having served aboard various vessels in different capacities. In 1694, Every became involved in a semi-legal venture known as privateering. Privateers were privately-owned ships granted government commissions to attack enemy ships during wartime, essentially legalized pirates. Every joined a privateering expedition under Captain Charles Gibson aboard the ship *Charles II* (also known as *Duke*).

The *Charles II* was part of an ambitious plan to seize Spanish ships in the Caribbean and off the coast of Africa. However, the expedition encountered numerous delays and hardships. Frustrated with their circumstances and lack of pay, the crew grew increasingly discontented. Every, who was the ship's first mate, capitalized on this dissatisfaction. On the night of May 7, 1694, he led a mutiny against Captain Gibson.

Every's leadership and charisma were crucial in convincing the crew to overthrow Gibson and seize the ship. Following the successful mutiny, Every was elected captain by his fellow sailors.

Renaming the ship *Fancy*, Every and his crew set out to become full-fledged pirates. The decision to turn pirate marked a critical juncture in Every's career. Unlike privateering, piracy was outright illegal and punishable by death. Every's crew accepted the risks in hopes of greater rewards. Under Every's command, the *Fancy* sailed towards the rich hunting grounds of the Indian Ocean, a region frequented by merchant vessels laden with valuable goods.

Every's most infamous exploit occurred in 1695, during what would later be known as the capture of the Mughal fleet. The Mughal Empire, one of the wealthiest and most powerful states in the world at the time, regularly sent fleets of ships on pilgrimages to Mecca. These ships carried immense wealth, including gold, silver, and precious stones. Every's decision to target this fleet was audacious and highly ambitious.

The climax of Every's career came in September 1695, off the coast of Surat in the Arabian Sea. Every's *Fancy* joined forces with several other pirate ships, including those commanded by Thomas Tew and Richard Want. Together, they intercepted and attacked the Mughal convoy. The most significant prize was the capture of the flagship, the *Ganj-i-Sawai* (also known as *Gunsway*), a massive and heavily armed ship. The *Ganj-i-Sawai* was carrying pilgrims returning from Mecca, as well as a fortune in treasure.

The battle for the *Ganj-i-Sawai* was fierce and bloody. Despite the ship's formidable defenses, the pirates ultimately prevailed. Accounts of the attack detail the brutal tactics used by Every's men, including the torture and murder of prisoners. The treasure seized from the *Ganj-i-Sawai* was immense, making Every and his crew incredibly wealthy. This raid was one of the most lucrative in the history of piracy, and its impact resonated far beyond the immediate spoils.

The repercussions of the attack on the *Ganj-i-Sawai* were profound. The Mughal Emperor Aurangzeb, enraged by the attack on his subjects and the desecration of his ships, demanded retribution. The British East India Company, which had extensive trading interests in India, faced severe backlash from the Mughal authorities. The company was compelled to make reparations and promise to bring Every to justice to restore its trading privileges and relations with the Mughal Empire.

Every and his crew, now extremely wealthy but also the most wanted men in the world, faced the daunting task of evading capture. They sailed westward, eventually arriving in the Caribbean. Knowing that ports in the New World were increasingly dangerous for pirates due to heightened efforts by colonial authorities to crack down on piracy, Every decided to disband his crew. He distributed the loot and suggested that his men go their separate ways to avoid drawing attention.

Every's crew dispersed across the Americas and Europe, but many were eventually captured and brought to trial. The trials of Every's men were highly publicized, reflecting the intense international pressure to punish those involved in the raid on the Mughal fleet. Several of Every's men were convicted and hanged, while others received lesser sentences or were acquitted due to lack of evidence or because they turned state's witness.

As for Henry Every himself, his fate remains one of the great mysteries of piracy. After disbanding his crew, Every seemingly vanished. There are numerous theories about what happened to him. Some suggest he lived out his days incognito in Britain, spending his fortune quietly. Others believe he may have assumed a new identity and lived in relative obscurity in the Caribbean or elsewhere. Despite extensive manhunts and a substantial bounty placed on his head by the British government, Every was never captured or definitively located.

His disappearance only added to his legendary status, fueling myths and stories that have persisted for centuries.

Every's legacy is multifaceted. He is often depicted as both a cunning and ruthless pirate who achieved immense success through audacity and brutality. The capture of the *Ganj-i-Sawai* remains one of the most significant pirate victories, showcasing the incredible risks and rewards associated with piracy during the Golden Age. Every's actions had far-reaching consequences, particularly for the British East India Company, which had to navigate the political fallout and repair its relations with the Mughal Empire.

The story of Henry Every also reflects broader themes in the history of piracy. His career illustrates the thin line between privateering and piracy, the appeal of immense wealth and freedom, and the harsh realities of life as an outlaw. Every's ability to evade capture and his mysterious end have cemented his place in the pantheon of legendary pirates, alongside figures like Blackbeard, Bartholomew Roberts, and William Kidd.

In popular culture, Every's story has been romanticized and mythologized, contributing to the enduring fascination with pirates. His exploits have been the subject of books, articles, and even fictionalized accounts in films and television. This fascination is not just due to his dramatic and lucrative raids, but also because of the air of mystery surrounding his ultimate fate.

Chapter 42: Christopher Moody

Christopher Moody is a figure from the Golden Age of Piracy whose career, while not as well-documented or infamous as some of his contemporaries, offers a fascinating glimpse into the life of an 18th-century pirate. His activities, marked by violence, strategic cunning, and a unique sense of pirate branding, provide valuable insights into the operational methods and social dynamics of pirate crews during this tumultuous period.

Christopher Moody's early life is shrouded in mystery, typical of many pirates of the era. Born around the 1690s, likely in England, there is little concrete information about his upbringing or the circumstances that led him to a life of piracy. It is assumed that, like many pirates, he began his maritime career on merchant or naval vessels, where he would have acquired the essential skills for navigation, seamanship, and combat. The harsh conditions and low pay typical of sailors during this time often pushed individuals towards piracy as a means of achieving wealth and autonomy.

Moody first appears in historical records in the early 18th century, a period marked by intense maritime activity and conflict. The War of Spanish Succession (1701-1714) and subsequent peace left many privateers unemployed, turning to piracy as a means of survival. While specific details of Moody's early piratical activities are sparse, he is believed to have been associated with several notable pirate captains, including Bartholomew Roberts, also known as Black Bart. This association is significant as Roberts was one of the most successful and feared pirates of the time, capturing over 400 ships during his career. Serving under Roberts would have provided Moody with invaluable experience and insights into the tactics and strategies of successful piracy.

Moody's rise to prominence as a pirate captain likely involved a combination of skill, audacity, and leadership. By the early 1720s, he had established himself as a formidable pirate commander, operating primarily in the Caribbean and the eastern coast of North America. The Caribbean was a hotspot for pirate activity due to its strategic location, busy shipping lanes, and numerous hiding spots among the islands. Moody, like many pirates of the era, took advantage of these conditions to launch attacks on merchant vessels.

One of the distinguishing features of Christopher Moody's career was his distinct approach to pirate branding. Unlike the typical black pirate flag, or Jolly Roger, which featured a skull and crossbones, Moody's flag was red and featured a skull, a heart dripping with blood, and an hourglass. The red flag, known as the "Bloody Red," was used to signal "no quarter," meaning no mercy would be shown to those who resisted. The addition of the hourglass symbolized the fleeting nature of life, emphasizing the imminent death awaiting Moody's victims if they did not surrender immediately. This unique branding served to instill fear and discourage resistance among the crews of targeted ships, enhancing Moody's fearsome reputation.

Moody's operational methods were typical of successful pirates of the time. He employed a combination of surprise attacks, overwhelming force, and psychological intimidation to capture ships with minimal resistance. His choice of targets included merchant vessels carrying valuable goods such as sugar, tobacco, and other commodities that were highly profitable in European markets. The wealth accumulated from these raids allowed Moody to maintain a well-armed and well-provisioned crew, essential for sustaining long-term piracy operations.

One of Moody's notable tactics was the use of speed and mobility. His ship, known for its swiftness, allowed him to chase down prey or evade naval patrols when necessary. Speed was a critical factor in pirate success, enabling quick attacks and rapid retreats before naval forces could respond effectively. Moody's ability to navigate the treacherous waters of the Caribbean and the Atlantic further enhanced his operational effectiveness, allowing him to exploit the vulnerabilities of his targets.

Despite his success, Moody's career was fraught with challenges typical of the pirate life. The early 18th century saw increasing efforts by colonial powers to suppress piracy, driven by the economic disruption and diplomatic tensions caused by pirate activities. The British, in particular, intensified their naval patrols and launched expeditions to capture or kill notorious pirates. This period saw the capture and execution of many prominent pirates, including Blackbeard and Bartholomew Roberts.

To evade capture, Moody and his crew adopted various strategies, including frequent relocation, utilization of hidden coves and islands for resupply and repairs, and maintaining a network of informants and allies among local populations. These measures, while effective to some extent, could not completely eliminate the constant threat of naval intervention. The increasing presence of naval forces in the Caribbean and the implementation of more sophisticated anti-piracy tactics made the pirate life increasingly perilous.

One of the most dramatic episodes in Moody's career was his encounter with a British naval squadron in the late 1720s. The details of this engagement are not fully documented, but it is believed that Moody's ship was cornered and a fierce battle ensued. Despite his tactical acumen and the ferocity of his crew, Moody's ship was heavily damaged. Demonstrating his resourcefulness, Moody managed to escape the immediate confrontation by navigating into shallow waters where the larger naval vessels could not follow. This narrow escape highlighted Moody's navigational skills and quick thinking but also underscored the growing dangers he faced.

Following this close call, Moody recognized the need for a more sustainable strategy to ensure his and his crew's survival. He sought to form alliances with other pirate captains and local privateers, creating a loose network of mutual support and information sharing. These alliances were crucial for resupplying, sharing intelligence about naval movements, and providing refuge in times of need. The cooperative approach also helped to distribute the risks and rewards of piracy more evenly, although maintaining such alliances required careful negotiation and trust-building.

The eventual fate of Christopher Moody is as enigmatic as his early life. Like many pirates, records of his later years are scant and often contradictory. Some sources suggest that he continued his piratical activities well into the 1730s, adapting to the changing circumstances and increasing naval pressure. Others imply that he may have sought a pardon or retired quietly, blending back into society to avoid capture. The lack of definitive information has contributed to the mystique surrounding Moody, allowing for various theories and legends to develop over time.

Moody's legacy in the annals of piracy is marked by his distinctive approach to branding, his strategic cunning, and his ability to adapt to the evolving threats of naval suppression. His career illustrates the complex interplay between piracy and legitimate maritime activities, highlighting how pirates exploited the vulnerabilities of global trade networks while also facing the relentless efforts of colonial powers to restore order on the high seas.

Christopher Moody's story also underscores the broader socio-economic context of the Golden Age of Piracy. The early 18th century was a period of significant maritime expansion, driven by the demands of European colonial empires for resources and wealth from the New World and other territories. This expansion created both opportunities and challenges for those who sought to operate outside the bounds of legality. Pirates like Moody navigated this complex landscape, balancing the allure of immense wealth with the constant threat of capture and execution.

In popular culture, Moody's unique pirate flag and his dramatic exploits have contributed to the enduring fascination with piracy. His story, though less well-known than some of his contemporaries, offers a rich narrative of daring, strategy, and survival that continues to captivate the imagination. The blend of historical fact and legend that surrounds Moody is emblematic of the broader cultural legacy of the Golden Age of Piracy, a period that has inspired countless books, films, and other media.

Chapter 43: James Bonney

James Bonney is a figure who occupies a rather shadowy corner in the annals of pirate history. Unlike the more famous buccaneers of the Golden Age of Piracy, such as Blackbeard or Bartholomew Roberts, Bonney's life and career are less well-documented, shrouded in mystery, and interspersed with a mix of legend and fact. This makes him an intriguing subject for historical inquiry and speculation. His nickname, "Deaf," suggests that he may have had a significant hearing impairment, which would have been a remarkable challenge for a seafarer in the tumultuous waters of the 17th century.

The exact details of Bonney's early life remain largely unknown, including his birth date and place. This is not uncommon for pirates of the era, many of whom emerged from obscurity and left few records behind. It is likely that Bonney, like many others who turned to piracy, started his maritime career in the merchant or naval services. The life of a sailor in the 17th century was fraught with hardship, low pay, and brutal discipline, which often drove men to seek the relative freedom and potential riches of piracy.

Bonney's transition to piracy would have been driven by a combination of economic necessity and the promise of wealth. The 17th century was a time of great maritime activity, with European powers vying for control of trade routes and colonies in the New World, Africa, and Asia. This environment created numerous opportunities for piracy, as merchant ships laden with valuable goods traversed the seas. Pirates like Bonney capitalized on these opportunities, using their knowledge of naval tactics and navigation to intercept and plunder these vessels.

One of the most significant aspects of Bonney's career was his association with other notable pirates. It is believed that he may have been connected to Anne Bonny, one of the most famous female pirates in history, though the exact nature of their relationship is unclear.

Some sources suggest that James Bonney could have been Anne's first husband, a small-time pirate himself, who played a role in introducing her to the world of piracy. Anne Bonny's later exploits alongside the infamous pirate John "Calico Jack" Rackham are well-documented, and her notoriety may have overshadowed any contributions James made to their shared history.

James "Deaf" Bonney's nickname implies that he had a hearing impairment, a significant obstacle in an era where communication, especially on a ship, relied heavily on spoken orders and signals. Despite this, Bonney appears to have managed to navigate the challenges posed by his condition, adapting to the harsh and demanding life at sea. His success as a pirate would have required exceptional resilience and ingenuity, as well as the ability to earn the respect and loyalty of his crew despite his disability.

The tactics and strategies employed by Bonney would have been similar to those of his contemporaries. Pirates of the 17th century relied on a combination of speed, surprise, and overwhelming force to capture their prey. They often used small, fast ships to outrun or outmaneuver larger, more heavily armed vessels. Once a target was identified, pirates would launch a swift and brutal attack, using grappling hooks to pull alongside the enemy ship and boarding it with cutlasses and pistols. The element of surprise was crucial, as was the ability to instill fear in their victims, who often surrendered without a fight to avoid the violence that typically accompanied resistance.

Bonney's activities would have taken place in a variety of maritime theaters, from the Caribbean to the Atlantic coast of North America and even the waters of the Indian Ocean. The Caribbean, in particular, was a hotbed of pirate activity due to its strategic location and the wealth of Spanish treasure fleets that passed through the region. Pirates like Bonney preyed on these rich targets, taking advantage of the region's numerous islands and hidden coves to evade capture and resupply their ships.

The life of a pirate was fraught with danger, not only from the inherent risks of their profession but also from the increasing efforts of colonial powers to suppress piracy. By the late 17th century, European nations were deploying more resources to combat the pirate threat, driven by the economic disruption and diplomatic tensions caused by pirate attacks on merchant shipping. Naval patrols were increased, and special commissions were established to hunt down and capture notorious pirates.

Despite these challenges, James "Deaf" Bonney managed to carve out a career as a pirate, although the specifics of his exploits remain largely undocumented. It is likely that he participated in numerous raids and engagements, seizing valuable cargoes and amassing a significant amount of wealth. Like many pirates, Bonney would have shared the spoils with his crew, maintaining morale and ensuring their loyalty through a combination of fair distribution of loot and charismatic leadership.

The eventual fate of James "Deaf" Bonney is as obscure as much of his life. Some accounts suggest that he may have met a violent end, either in battle or through execution if captured by colonial authorities. Others speculate that he might have taken advantage of the various pardons offered to pirates during periods of intensified anti-piracy efforts, retiring quietly and disappearing from historical records. The lack of concrete evidence allows for a wide range of interpretations and theories, contributing to the enduring mystique surrounding his figure.

The legacy of James "Deaf" Bonney, though less prominent than that of more famous pirates, is nonetheless significant in the broader context of pirate history. His career illustrates the diversity and adaptability of pirates during the Golden Age of Piracy, highlighting the ways in which individuals with unique challenges, such as a hearing impairment, could still achieve success and notoriety. Bonney's story also underscores the pervasive allure of piracy in the 17th century, driven by the promise of wealth, adventure, and a rejection of the harsh conditions faced by legitimate sailors.

In popular culture, the figure of James "Deaf" Bonney has not received the same level of attention as other pirates, yet his story adds depth and variety to the rich tapestry of pirate lore. The combination of mystery, adversity, and potential connections to more famous pirates like Anne Bonny makes him a compelling subject for further exploration in literature, film, and historical research.

Overall, James "Deaf" Bonney's life and career offer a fascinating glimpse into the world of 17th-century piracy, characterized by daring exploits, strategic cunning, and the relentless pursuit of freedom and fortune. His story, though fragmented and elusive, contributes to our understanding of the diverse individuals who navigated the treacherous waters of the Golden Age of Piracy, leaving an indelible mark on history and continuing to inspire curiosity and fascination today.

Chapter 44: John Halsey

John Halsey, active in the early 18th century, was a notorious pirate whose life and exploits left a significant mark on the history of piracy during its Golden Age. Born in the 1680s, Halsey's career encapsulates the turbulent dynamics of the maritime world during this period. His journey from a legitimate privateer to a feared pirate underscores the fluid boundaries between legality and criminality that characterized the era. Despite the lack of detailed records about his early life, Halsey's piratical activities in the Atlantic and Indian Oceans provide a rich narrative of adventure, cunning, and maritime prowess.

John Halsey is believed to have been born in New England, a region with a burgeoning maritime culture and economy. The details of his early life remain obscure, but it is likely that he gained seafaring experience as a young man, which prepared him for his future ventures. By the early 1700s, Halsey had established himself as a privateer. Privateering, a practice sanctioned by governments, allowed private individuals to arm ships and attack enemy vessels during wartime, sharing the spoils with their sponsors. This quasi-legal form of piracy blurred the lines between lawful combatants and outlaws, providing a legitimate cover for many who would later turn to outright piracy.

Halsey's career as a privateer began in the context of the War of Spanish Succession (1701-1714), a major conflict involving several European powers. The war created opportunities for privateers to profit from attacking enemy ships, particularly those of Spain and France. Halsey received a privateering commission from the British government, allowing him to target Spanish and French vessels legally. His early successes as a privateer would have provided him with valuable experience in naval combat and a taste for the lucrative rewards of maritime predation.

The transition from privateer to pirate was a common trajectory for many seafarers of the time. As the War of Spanish Succession drew to a close, the demand for privateers diminished, leaving many former privateers without employment. The cessation of hostilities also meant the revocation of privateering commissions, pushing men like Halsey toward piracy to maintain their livelihoods. By the early 1700s, Halsey had abandoned his privateering commission and embraced a life of piracy.

Halsey began his piratical career in the Atlantic, targeting merchant ships traveling between Europe, Africa, and the Americas. He quickly gained a reputation for his boldness and tactical skill. His operations extended into the Indian Ocean, a region that had become increasingly popular among pirates due to its rich trade routes and the wealth of East India Company vessels. The Indian Ocean's vast expanse and numerous islands provided ideal conditions for pirate activity, allowing Halsey and his crew to evade capture and strike at lucrative targets.

One of Halsey's most notable exploits occurred in the early 1700s when he captured a large Portuguese ship off the coast of Africa. The ship, laden with valuable cargo, provided a substantial haul for Halsey and his crew. This victory not only demonstrated his naval prowess but also underscored the international nature of piracy, where ships of various nationalities were fair game. The capture of the Portuguese vessel bolstered Halsey's reputation and attracted more men to his crew, eager to share in the spoils.

Halsey's success in the Indian Ocean was due in part to his strategic alliances and his ability to exploit local geopolitical dynamics. He formed temporary alliances with other pirate captains, pooling resources and coordinating attacks to maximize their effectiveness. These alliances were often short-lived, driven by immediate mutual interests rather than long-term loyalty. The fluid and opportunistic nature of pirate alliances reflected the precarious and competitive environment in which they operated.

The pirates of the Indian Ocean faced significant challenges, not least of which was the threat posed by the powerful navies of European colonial powers. The British, French, and Portuguese all had vested interests in protecting their lucrative trade routes and colonial holdings. To counter these threats, Halsey and his fellow pirates employed hit-and-run tactics, using their knowledge of local waters and the element of surprise to their advantage. They also relied on the support of local populations, who were often willing to trade with pirates for goods and services at lower prices than those offered by official channels.

Halsey's career as a pirate was marked by a series of high-profile captures and daring escapades. In one notable incident, he and his crew seized a large Armenian ship carrying a rich cargo of silk and spices. The capture of such valuable goods demonstrated Halsey's ability to target high-value ships and avoid detection by naval forces. His success in the Indian Ocean attracted the attention of colonial authorities, who were increasingly determined to stamp out piracy in the region.

Despite his successes, Halsey's career was not without its setbacks. The harsh conditions of pirate life, including battles, disease, and the constant threat of capture, took their toll on him and his crew. In one instance, Halsey's ship was severely damaged in a storm, forcing him to seek refuge and repair his vessel. Such challenges were part and parcel of the pirate's existence, requiring resilience and adaptability.

Halsey's operations eventually drew the ire of the British East India Company, which was determined to protect its interests in the region. The company, backed by the British government, launched a concerted campaign to hunt down and eliminate pirates in the Indian Ocean. The increasing presence of naval patrols and the offer of pardons to pirates willing to surrender put pressure on Halsey and his contemporaries.

Faced with mounting challenges, Halsey sought to negotiate his way out of piracy. He approached the British authorities, offering to surrender in exchange for a pardon. Such negotiations were not uncommon, as colonial powers often saw the benefit of reintegrating experienced seafarers into legitimate roles. The outcome of Halsey's negotiations remains unclear, with some accounts suggesting he may have retired quietly, while others propose he continued his piratical activities under a different guise.

John Halsey's later years are shrouded in mystery, with scant records detailing his fate. It is believed that he may have returned to New England or sought refuge in another part of the world. The lack of definitive information about his later life and death has fueled speculation and legend, adding to the enigmatic nature of his legacy.

Halsey's life as a pirate reflects broader themes in the history of piracy during the Golden Age. His ability to transition from a legitimate privateer to a feared pirate highlights the thin line between lawful and unlawful maritime activities. The economic and political turmoil of the early 18th century created an environment in which piracy could flourish, driven by the opportunities for wealth and the challenges of post-war unemployment.

Halsey's strategic acumen and his ability to forge alliances underscore the sophisticated nature of pirate operations. Far from being mere outlaws, pirates like Halsey demonstrated a keen understanding of naval tactics, commerce, and diplomacy. Their activities were embedded in the broader geopolitical context of their time, influencing and being influenced by the actions of colonial powers and global trade networks.

The legacy of John Halsey, like that of many pirates, is a blend of fact and fiction. His exploits have been romanticized in literature and popular culture, where he is often depicted as a daring and cunning rogue. Such portrayals capture the enduring allure of the pirate archetype, characterized by adventure, rebellion, and a defiance of conventional authority.

In historical terms, Halsey's life offers valuable insights into the complexities of piracy and privateering in the early 18th century. His career illustrates the fluidity of maritime identities and the interplay between legality and criminality. The impact of his actions on trade and colonial security highlights the significance of piracy as a force that shaped the economic and political landscape of the time.

172

Chapter 45: Benjamin Hornigold

Benjamin Hornigold, born in the 1680s and active until his death in 1719, stands as one of the most prominent and influential pirates of the Golden Age of Piracy. His career, marked by significant contributions to the pirate community and complex interactions with colonial authorities, offers a comprehensive look into the life of a pirate during this tumultuous period. Hornigold's legacy includes not only his own exploits but also his mentorship of other legendary pirates, such as Edward Teach, better known as Blackbeard.

The exact details of Benjamin Hornigold's early life are largely unknown, but it is generally believed he was born in England in the 1680s. His maritime career likely began in the merchant or naval services, common starting points for many who would later turn to piracy. By the early 18th century, Hornigold had gravitated towards the Bahamas, a region that would become central to his piratical activities.

The Bahamas, particularly the island of New Providence, was a hotbed of piracy during the early 1700s. The island's strategic location near major shipping routes and its lack of effective colonial governance made it an ideal base for pirates. New Providence's harbor, with its deep waters and natural defenses, provided a safe haven for pirate ships to refit and resupply. It was in this environment that Hornigold began to make a name for himself as a pirate captain.

By 1713, Hornigold had established himself as a formidable pirate leader. His early exploits primarily involved targeting Spanish ships, capitalizing on the longstanding hostilities between Spain and England. Hornigold's tactics were typical of the era, relying on speed, surprise, and intimidation to capture vessels and plunder their cargoes. He often spared the crews of captured ships, a practice that helped maintain a reputation for fairness and attracted skilled seamen to his crew.

One of Hornigold's significant contributions to piracy was his role in the formation of the "Republic of Pirates" on New Providence Island. This informal pirate haven was characterized by a loose confederation of pirate captains who governed themselves through a code of conduct and mutual agreement. The absence of colonial authority allowed these pirates to operate with relative impunity, creating a thriving community based on shared interests and collective defense.

Hornigold's leadership and organizational skills were instrumental in the success of the pirate haven. He was known for his ability to maintain discipline and order among his crew, essential qualities for the survival and efficiency of pirate operations. His fair treatment of his men and his adherence to the pirate code earned him respect and loyalty, making him one of the leading figures in the pirate community.

A pivotal aspect of Hornigold's legacy is his mentorship of other prominent pirates, most notably Edward Teach, who would become infamous as Blackbeard. Teach joined Hornigold's crew around 1716, and under Hornigold's tutelage, he honed the skills and tactics that would later make him one of the most feared pirates of all time. The relationship between Hornigold and Teach exemplifies the hierarchical and apprenticeship nature of pirate crews, where experienced captains would train and mold future leaders.

Hornigold's piracy was not solely motivated by personal gain; he was also driven by a sense of patriotism and a desire to undermine Spain's influence in the Caribbean. This sentiment was reflected in his choice of targets, primarily Spanish and French ships, which aligned with British interests. This quasi-patriotic stance made him somewhat distinct among pirates, many of whom were driven purely by profit.

By 1717, the British government, alarmed by the increasing threat posed by pirates, launched a concerted effort to suppress piracy in the Atlantic and Caribbean. The arrival of Woodes Rogers as the governor of the Bahamas marked a turning point in the fight against piracy. Rogers was tasked with restoring order to the islands and eradicating the pirate threat. One of his strategies was to offer a royal pardon to any pirate who would renounce their criminal ways and pledge allegiance to the Crown.

Hornigold, recognizing the changing tides, decided to accept the pardon offered by Rogers. His decision was likely influenced by several factors, including the increasing pressure from naval forces, the dwindling opportunities for successful piracy, and his own pragmatic nature. By accepting the pardon, Hornigold avoided the harsh punishments that awaited those who continued their piratical activities.

After accepting the pardon, Hornigold took on a new role as a pirate hunter. His intimate knowledge of pirate tactics and hideouts made him an invaluable asset to Rogers in the campaign against his former comrades. Hornigold's shift from pirate-to-pirate hunter illustrates the fluidity of allegiance and the complex moral landscape of the time. His actions as a pirate hunter further cemented his legacy, showcasing his adaptability and strategic acumen.

Hornigold's efforts as a pirate hunter were met with mixed success. While he was able to capture several pirates and disrupt their operations, his former association with the pirate community led to accusations of leniency and favoritism. Despite these challenges, Hornigold's contributions to the suppression of piracy were significant, helping to restore a measure of order to the region.

In 1719, Hornigold met his end in a hurricane near New Spain (modern-day Mexico). His death marked the close of a career that had spanned the full spectrum of piracy, from rogue captain to reformed pirate hunter. The exact circumstances of his death remain unclear, but it is generally believed that his ship was caught in the storm and wrecked, leading to his demise.

Benjamin Hornigold's legacy is multifaceted, reflecting the complexity of the pirate world during the Golden Age of Piracy. He was a skilled and daring pirate captain, a respected leader in the pirate haven of New Providence, and a pragmatic figure who navigated the shifting allegiances of his time. His mentorship of Blackbeard and other pirates ensured that his influence extended beyond his own career, shaping the next generation of pirates.

Hornigold's life also highlights the broader themes of piracy in the early 18th century. The economic and political instability of the period, combined with the opportunities for wealth and adventure on the high seas, created an environment in which piracy could thrive. The blurred lines between privateering and piracy, and the fluid nature of pirate allegiances, underscore the complexities of maritime law and order during this time.

Hornigold's role in the establishment and governance of the Republic of Pirates on New Providence Island offers valuable insights into the self-organizing capabilities of pirate communities. These havens were not lawless free-for-alls but rather societies governed by codes of conduct and mutual agreements, reflecting a form of proto-democratic governance that stood in contrast to the autocratic rule of colonial powers.

In popular culture, Benjamin Hornigold has been depicted in various ways, from a ruthless pirate to a pragmatic leader. His story has inspired numerous books, films, and video games, cementing his place in the pantheon of legendary pirates. These portrayals, while often romanticized, capture the enduring fascination with the adventurous and rebellious spirit of pirates.

Epilogue

The world of piracy, with its turbulent seas and relentless pursuit of freedom, has long since faded into the annals of history. The era of the historical pirates, marked by the bold exploits and daring adventures of the men and women chronicled in this book, now serves as a powerful reminder of a time when the boundaries between law and lawlessness were as fluid as the tides.

From Klaus Störtebeker's audacious raids in the North Sea to Cheng I Sao's dominance over the South China Sea, the stories of these pirates reveal a common thread: a yearning for autonomy in a world dictated by empires and economies. Their lives, often brutal and brief, were spent challenging the status quo, seeking fortune, and navigating the perilous line between legend and infamy.

In revisiting the lives of these historical pirates, we uncover more than just tales of maritime plunder. We find complex characters, shaped by the socio-political landscapes of their times, who dared to defy the norms. Grace O'Malley's defiance of English rule, Henry Morgan's transformation from pirate to privateer, and Blackbeard's reign of terror along the American coast all reflect the diverse motivations and legacies that define piracy.

The stories of pirates like Anne Bonny and Mary Read disrupt the conventional narratives of gender, showcasing women who fought and led alongside their male counterparts, challenging the rigid gender roles of their era. Their tales of courage and defiance continue to inspire and intrigue, highlighting the often-overlooked contributions of women in the world of piracy.

The exploits of Francis Drake and Peter Easton remind us of the thin line between heroism and villainy, a line that was often drawn based on perspective and allegiance. While celebrated by some as heroes and patriots, others viewed them as ruthless marauders. This duality underscores the complexity of piracy and the shifting moral landscapes of the time.

As we reach the end of this journey through the lives of these historical pirates, it is clear that their legacy extends far beyond the loot they plundered or the ships they commandeered. They have become symbols of rebellion and freedom, their stories enduring in the cultural imagination. Through literature, film, and folklore, the mythos of the pirate continues to captivate, reminding us of the human spirit's unending quest for adventure and autonomy.

The age of sail has long since given way to modern technology, and the wooden ships that once roamed the seas have been replaced by steel giants. Yet, the stories of these pirates remain as a testament to an era when the oceans were a frontier, and those who dared to challenge its depths became legends.

In the end, the historical pirates were more than outlaws; they were pioneers of a different kind, navigating a world of uncertainty with a determination that has left an indelible mark on history. Their tales, filled with triumphs and tragedies, continue to echo across the centuries, reminding us of the enduring allure of the sea and the timeless quest for freedom.

As we close this book, let us remember the historical pirates not just as figures of a distant past, but as enduring symbols of courage, defiance, and the relentless pursuit of a life unbound by the ordinary. Their stories, forever etched in the pages of history, remind us that the spirit of adventure and the desire for freedom are as boundless as the seas they once sailed.

The End.

www.ingramcontent.com/pod-product-compliance
Lightning Source LLC
Chambersburg PA
CBHW031044160726
47991CB00005B/2020